Acknowledgements

Thanks to Andy Spellman for sticking it out, Gary Inman for translating, Nigel the dog just for being there and to Sharon for squaring me up. And thanks to everyone for finding my life interesting enough to read about.

GUY MARTIN

WORMS TO CATCH

Virgin BOOKS

1 3 5 7 9 10 8 6 4 2

Virgin Books, an imprint of Ebury Publishing,
20 Vauxhall Bridge Road,
London SW1V 2SA

Virgin Books is part of the Penguin Random House group of
companies whose addresses can be found at
global.penguinrandomhouse.com

Penguin
Random House
UK

First published by Virgin Books in 2016

www.penguin.co.uk

A CIP catalogue record for this book is available from the
British Library

HB ISBN 9780753545300
TPB ISBN 9780753545317

Designed and typeset by K.DESIGN, Winscombe, Somerset
Printed and bound in Great Britain by Clays Ltd, St Ives PLC

Penguin Random House is committed to a sustainable future for our
business, our readers and our planet. This book is made from Forest
Stewardship Council® certified paper

CONTENTS

CHAPTER 1

All I could blame it on was the motorcycles

THIS TIME LAST year, August 2015, I was in a Belfast hospital, and all I could think was, It's going to be a few weeks of lying about before I get back to normal. I wasn't bothered about the pain, but I couldn't stand the thought of being forced to lie about. I'd crashed my

BMW S1000RR leading a race at the Ulster Grand Prix and broken my back and my hand. It was the second time I'd broken my spine crashing a motorbike in just over five years, and I'd got away without too much lasting damage. I had a big scar up my back, where they'd cut me open to bolt my spine together, and some more new metalwork in my hand. Bloody lucky really, but all I could blame it on was the motorcycles.

I'd been thinking and talking about the Tour Divide, a 2,745-mile mountain-bike race in Canada and America, for ages, and it became something to focus on instead of motorbikes, for a while at least. I would compete in that the following June. I also decided I wouldn't commit to any road races until after the Tour Divide, mainly because even a small injury would knacker up my training. I thought that all those hours on my own, cycling from the top to the bottom of America, would be the perfect time to think about me and motorbikes. Racing had been a way of life for 15 years, more or less, and if I did pack them in it wasn't going to be because of a snap decision.

The wall of death record attempt had to be cancelled because of the back injury too. The date hadn't been decided 100 per cent, but it was going to be in October. It would have been a hell of a job to get the Rob North Triumph finished for then. I'd have done it, I reckon, but it wouldn't have been as good as I'd hoped.

My diary was clear all of a sudden – there's only so much you can do with a broken back – but I was determined that it wasn't going to slow me up for long. And plenty of folk did a good job of filling it back up, but not straight away.

For a week after the crash I was laid up in the hospital, then I got home and had another week of not being able to do much. I was hardly sleeping. I'd already finished *When You Dead, You Dead*, and it was on its way to the printers, but the end needed a bit of a rewrite to include what had happened at the Ulster. It seemed a bit daft to have had this potentially life-changing crash and not mention it in the book if we could squeeze it in. And we did.

Then I went back to work. The first day in the truck yard I was useless. I was in so much pain I couldn't do anything. I fitted a door handle on a truck and that was it, I had to come home. I couldn't lift my arms up. The next day I went in, and that was a bit better. I put a header tank in a Scania 730 and that's a bugger to do because you have to take loads of stuff off to get access to it. It's a five-hour job when I'm fit, and I thought to myself, If I can do that by the end of the week, I'll be alright. I gave myself four full days, but I managed it in a day with time left to do another small job, so I was pleased with that.

My boss, Mick Moody was glad to see me back and he was brilliant. He explained what we needed to do at work and asked, 'What do you reckon?' There were some things I couldn't manage at first. I couldn't handle the big windy gun, so Moody would come do that if I got stuck. He was spot on. One day I was putting an air filter in a wagon. I had to lie on my back at the side of the pit, the big hole in the ground that the lorries park over so you can work under the truck, and reach up to push this air filter into place. It's not heavy, but it's awkward. And that movement, laying on my back, pushing something away from my chest, hurt so much I squealed like a girl. Moody could hear me in his office, 100 yards away across the yard, and came to see what was up. 'Are you alright?' he asked. I told him I was a bit sore, but I would be. I think it was so painful because the muscles weren't attached – they'd been cut off when the metalwork was bolted to my spine – and I was asking them to do something they weren't ready for. But I fitted the filter in the end. It probably took me ten times longer than normal, but I did do it.

I started thinking about getting back on my pushbike as early as the first few days back at work, so not even three weeks after the break. I'd get up at five o'clock, because I always have worms to catch, get my bike out and cycle as far as the end of the village, half a mile away, before admitting to myself, 'Bastard, I can't do this,' and turning back for home. Even though I was on my mountain bike, which is comfier than the Rourke bike I normally ride to work on, I still couldn't hack it. The rucksack on my back was hurting and everything was still sore as hell. I'd come home, take the dog for a bit of a walk, have another cup of tea and then drive the van in.

The second week, I managed to bike in one way, then I got a lift home with Belty, Moody's valeter, who lives near me. Then I'd do that again, one way, and by the end of the week I was sometimes biking both ways. Only writing this makes me remember the pain, otherwise all I'd remember about the aftermath of the accident is the inconvenience.

My girlfriend Sharon and my mum and dad thought I'd gone back to work too early, but a week later Sharon could see it was good for me and knew I was coming along loads faster than if I'd stayed laying on the sofa. For me it's the right thing. I wasn't trying to be a hero or anything, but I needed to prove I could still do it. I wasn't down – I don't think I ever get down. And I was off the painkillers after the first week. They put me on tramadol and I was supposed to be taking four a day, but I'd had trouble with them when I'd broken my back at the TT in 2010. I was addicted to them for a short while and I didn't want to go down that road again, so I gritted my teeth instead.

I wrote in the introduction to the last book, 'Why another one?' I wondered the same before starting this one, but there's a demand. People like reading them, and I like writing them. I can imagine reading them in ten years and it bringing back a load of memories. I like reading and the book people reckoned that a lot of folk who bought the last two books weren't big book buyers, so if mine get people reading and that maybe even leads them to a bit of George Orwell or Aldous Huxley then I think that's great.

I thought packing in road racing, at least until after the Tour Divide, would let me have more time to myself, but it's been the opposite, so there's plenty to write about. I've had a right exciting year. Every year I wonder, How is this year going to top the last? But it always does. Every year seems madder than the previous one. So, thanks very much for buying the book. I hope you enjoy it.

CHAPTER 2

Kaspars is a blind Latvian MOT inspector

THE ULSTER CRASH only kept me out of the truck yard for a couple of weeks, but it did scupper some big stuff I was looking forward to, including the attempt to set the fastest ever speed on a wall of death, which was meant to be shown live on the telly before Christmas. Every year deals way beyond my level of involvement are made between North One, the production company I've always worked with, and Channel 4, about delivering programmes. Now that the wall of death wasn't going to happen for a good few months the TV bods were looking for something else to fill the gap. Making the travel programme about India felt like a big commitment, going out there for a fortnight, but I enjoyed it and it went down well. So North One said, 'Why don't we do another travel programme? Where do you want to go?'

I'm not the kind of traveller who goes places to say they've been there. I'm not a box-ticker – I want a good reason to visit somewhere. I've always been interested in communism, so I went to Cuba a few years back to see all that before it ended, and I went to Croatia before it changed and became too westernised.

I came up with Latvia, because of my granddad on my mum's side, Voldemars 'Walter' Kidals. It was going on for ten years since Walter had died. I knew he'd had a fascinating life, being forced to fight for the Nazis in the Second World War before escaping, becoming a prisoner of war and eventually ending up married to Double-Decker Lil in North Lincolnshire. But there was a lot the family didn't know. Walter was a quiet man. He wasn't unfriendly – he'd take me into the shed and show me what he was up to, take us to see his sheep and chickens. And I used Walter's thoughts on the afterlife – when you dead, you dead – for the name of my last book.

They said. 'Latvia? Right then! We'll do some research.' I'm not blowing my own trumpet, but the TV lot are dead keen for me to make programmes. They'd have twice as many, if I wanted to do them, so when we agree to do summat that we're both happy with, things start moving quickly.

Walter and Lil had four sons and a daughter, the daughter being my mum, Rita. The relative who knew the most about Walter was my uncle John, my mum's younger brother. My mum knew a bit, but my dad probably knew more than her because he talked to Walter about his past more than my mum did. But no one knew the whole picture or, as it turned out, anything close to the whole picture. Uncle John was the main contact and he put the TV lot in touch with the other side of the family in Latvia, and research discovered stuff that we would never have found out.

I was dead interested to see what we were going to learn when I flew with the TV crew from Luton to Riga, the capital of Latvia, on 29 October. Ahead of us was a week and a bit of travelling around the country, looking into what Walter had done in Latvia before leaving and why he came to England, and seeing what we could find out about his family.

I'd been given some books on the history of the country, and I read that every man and his dog had had a go at ruling Latvia. Back in the thirteenth century some German warrior monks were in charge. I'm not sure what a warrior monk is, but they sound dead cool. I'd like to see Quentin Tarantino have a stab at making a film about German warrior monks. By the sixteenth century, Poles and Lithuanians had taken over. The Swedes were running the job in the seventeenth century, then it was the Russians' turn.

After the First World War the Latvians finally got their independence, and it all sounded good for the country, but it only lasted for 25 years. As the world watched Hitler's army invade Poland and then France, the Russians rolled into Latvia and took all the privately owned goods and services into state ownership.

My first impression of Riga was that everything looked very new, giving me the feeling it had been built with EU money. But there was a medieval part of Riga too, and we visited the huge indoor market, the biggest in Europe, which is housed in old hangars built for Zeppelins in the 1920s. I liked the city.

The TV lot had found something for me to drive around in, a Russian-built Lada 1300 S, the perfect car for the job, especially as it was the same age as me – a 1981 model. The bloke who we borrowed it from reckoned it had been used as a rally car. His name was Kaspars, and he was based in Strazdumuiža, about half an hour out of Riga. We were told that Kaspars was a blind Latvian

MOT inspector. He was legendary in the area for being dead good with cars, even though he had this disability. I was impressed, and wondered how he could work on cars for a living if he couldn't see what he was doing. I watched as he felt his way around the car, so I had no doubt that he was blind until I turned around and he was texting on his phone. The TV bods cracked up with laughter, but we were trying to keep it in, because we didn't want him to think we were laughing at him. The Lada showed up in the TV programme, but Kaspars didn't. I think he might have been on the fiddle.

I met with Dr Aleks Feigmanis, a family-tree specialist, who looked through loads of records to find out anything he could about my granddad and his family. We sat behind a table with big, old ledger-type books giving details of births and other moments in Walter's life. I'm not the tallest, but the researcher wasn't a big lad, and he asked to sit on a cushion to look a bit taller. No bother, mate.

The earliest record of the relevant Kidals was in the 1835 census. Aleks found out that I'm a descendant of the Curonians, who he described as a brave tribe of ruthless pirates who went to war with the Vikings. He told me that church bells had inscriptions saying 'Save us from God and Curonians'.

In 1853, my great-great-granddad was in the Russian army, at a time when service was a minimum of 25 years. It was also during the period of the Crimean War.

We learned that my granddad's first name wasn't even Voldemars – it was Janis. Voldemars was his middle name. We can only guess why he changed it, and if I had to I'd say it was because he wanted a new start when he eventually reached England. Research showed that Voldemars grew up in a rural village called Asite (pronounced Ass-E-tay), and records listed Walter as growing up in a school. The expert reckoned the most likely reason for that was because he'd been orphaned. He was born in 1920 and we knew he hadn't had an easy life, by any measure, but none of our family knew that about him. I set off in the Lada to see what I could see.

Asite was right out in the sticks, a four-hour drive and a lot of it on dirt roads. We found the school, but it was explained to us that it looked a lot different to how it would have when Walter was there in the early 1930s. The Russians had dismantled part of it for materials to build other stuff. Now it was a house with an old couple living in it. They were happy for us to look around.

Asite used to have a population of 2,500 people. There were 319 farms in the area, smallholdings I suppose, and a couple of windmills, but it was caught in the middle of the fighting on the Eastern Front in 1944 and was totally flattened. I met an old forest ranger called Sigurd, who remembered the time when Walter lived there, though he didn't remember Walter. Aleks had told us the name of the farm where my granddad was born, and Sigurd had a 90-year-old hunting map he used to show us exactly where Walter grew up before he was orphaned.

We searched for it and found a few stones that we thought could be from the old farmhouse. Uncle John had told us that Voldemars had said he used to enjoy going to a nearby church, and we found the remains of it. It had been built in 1700 or thereabouts, but it was in ruins from the Second World War. It was emotional to see where he'd come from.

The war would change every Latvian's life. The country was invaded three times in quick succession. In June 1940, when the Russians rolled in, anyone who stood up to them was sent to the Gulag – the Russian forced-labour camps that few ever got out of alive.

Latvians called that time the Year of Terror. Understandably, most hated the communists. The Russians and Germans had a pre-war agreement that they wouldn't tread on each other's toes, but Hitler sent his troops into Latvia. They chased the Russians out with not much bother, and the Nazis were welcomed with open arms, because the locals hated the Russians so much. Little did they know. With the help of extreme right-wing Latvians, the Nazis went after the Jewish population, killing 25,000 in just two nights. Around 80,000 Latvian Jews were killed in total, and nearly a third of the population of the country fled or were killed or deported over this time.

The Germans started conscripting Latvians to fight against Britain and its allies. The family already knew Walter had been conscripted into the Waffen-SS, but we found out more during a visit to the Latvian War Museum. Military history expert Jānis Tomaševskis told me that if anyone said they wouldn't fight for the Germans not only would they be punished, but they risked their family being sent to the labour camps too. Walter was trained as a gunner in the 19th Artillery Division, but then his name showed up as being part of the infantry, the cannon fodder. It took a while to train a gunner, so it sounds like he was transferred to the infantry as a punishment, probably for deserting. We went to see a war re-enactment – Germans versus the Russians – and I was nervous when the bombs started going off, with tanks and half-tracks churning up the countryside and dummy rounds being fired.

Uncle John knew a few bits that his dad had told him about his time in the army – seeing his mate being taken out by a sniper, and marching along roads lined with people crucified at the side of the road. So we knew, or had a good idea, he had deserted and been captured by the Germans and sent to the front line, where he was lucky not to have been killed. Then he was captured by the Americans and sent to a camp in Belgium as a prisoner of war. Many Latvians were only fighting for the Germans because the alternative was execution.

They used to say that they'd deal with the Russians first, then turn on the Germans. But the Americans only saw soldiers in Nazi uniforms. They didn't know, or care, about the story of the Latvian conscripts, so it wasn't until 1947, two years after the end of the war, that Walter was released and was no longer a prisoner of war. He was put on a boat set for Canada, but when it stopped in England he didn't go any further. He met my grandma, Double-Decker Lil, in October 1951, and they married the following March.

We saw a lot of Latvia as we travelled from one location to the next, and I liked the place. It was quiet, no hustle and bustle – a bit backwards. Like Lincolnshire. It's not known for much. It's over the Baltic Sea from Sweden and has Lithuania below and Estonia above, with Russia on the eastern border. We drove around an area north of a city called Liepāja, the third biggest in Latvia, on the coast. Every building seemed to be one of those dead square Soviet blocks of flats, and all of them looked like they were slowly dropping to bits. It wasn't a shithole, but it had seen better days, and even those days might not have been that good. On the beach were concrete bunkers that we did some filming around.

One night in Liepāja, I was taken to a hotel that used to be an old prison. Built in 1905, Karosta Prison dates back to the days of the tsars, before the revolution and communist rule, and was originally a naval prison. In the

Soviet days the KGB – the secret police – took over. Now the prison is described as the worst hotel in Europe. I don't know why they left it at Europe – I don't think any hotel in the world could be as bad. If there is one, they're doing something really wrong. Karosta advertises to stag and hen dos and those management-bonding groups, so they can experience being treated like a prisoner in the Cold War era.

I walked into the courtyard and approached a guard to get checked in. I went to shake his hand but he smacked it away, so I knew where I stood. Or I thought I did. As soon as I went through the door I was battered and knocked about. The guard was screaming at me in Russian, but I obviously had no clue what he was saying. At first I thought it was a bit of an act, but the longer it went on the more I thought, These buggers aren't messing. I was put up against the wall to be searched and the guard found something in my pocket. He asked what it was, or I thought he did, because he was growling at me in Russian. I took my wallet out of my front jeans pocket to show him, and he snatched it out of my hand and chucked it.

I had to do an assault course, then I was put in all these stress positions that are used on prisoners of war and Guantanamo detainees as a form of torture. You put your arms behind you head and squat low to the floor, staying there until they say move.

Then the guards took me to a cell where I was shown how to make my bed. If you don't make it exactly how the guard wants it, he chucks it against the wall and starts pushing you about. And he was a big unit. He wasn't messing. I had to keep telling him something that sounded like 'Tes Toyshna'. I reckon it meant 'Yes, sir'.

The TV lot thought the experience would be a bit more 'play fighting' for the camera, but it wasn't. I was expecting a bit of a banter and some gruel, and even thought about bringing my book to read in the cell. I was way off. The Russian voice was intimidating enough, but it wasn't long after I'd broken my back and being shoved about and booted when I was on the floor was a bit much. The wall of death had been cancelled because they reckoned I wasn't fit to ride a bike and the insurance company wouldn't sign me off, but here I was in a Russian prison getting the shit kicked out of me on a cold concrete floor by a Latvian nutter. I wasn't wimping out, but my self-preservation kicked in and I lifted up my top to show the fresh pink scar running the length of my spine, as if to say, Come on, mate.

I had meant to stay the night, but I didn't in the end. I was still hurting too much, so we went back to this rare hotel, the Fontaine, in the same coastal town of Liepāja. It was no bother getting in. The town was quiet when we were there, out of season, at the beginning of November.

I liked the place, because the reception doubled up as a shop where I bought a Russian gas mask and a poster that's on the wall at home.

The last job before coming home was to meet all the family. Walter had two brothers, Arvids and Rihards and their two sides of the family tree had never met each other. There was no friction between the families I met, but I think there might have been between Walter's two brothers. The Kidals family came from all over the country to meet in a pub, just outside of Riga.

I was dead nervous about meeting them. I thought it was going to be like pulling teeth, with painful small talk, but it was spot on. They were nice people. They all spoke English, some perfectly, and I learned that one of my relations opened the first disco in Latvia and owned a lighting company that supplied nightclubs and shops. One relative was a tree surgeon, and another worked in a launderette. One lass was an English teacher whose two sons were in university, one of them in Switzerland. Her son, Uldis, said they could tell straight away I was a Kidals, because of my 'square head, side beards, big nose and eyes set back in my head'.

We flew home on 8 November, and the main thing that stayed with me was how hard Walter's life had been. I knew before that he hadn't had it easy, but I had no idea just how much he'd been through. My mum was upset because she hadn't understood how tough his life had been before he reached England. There was no wonder he could be a bit of an awkward bugger.

He was one of 26,000 what they termed 'displaced' persons – now called immigrants – who came from Latvia to the UK to work. A report from the time in the local Hull paper said they were here to do the dirty jobs the English people will not look at, adding, 'They are likely to show up the British workforce with their likeliness to work hard.' And this was in 1947, telling a country that had worked its balls off to survive the war! And I think they were right. The Latvians would do anything to get out from under Soviet control. Walter only ever went back twice because he was fearful of what the Russians might do. He took my mum in 1979, and she remembers them being warned to be careful about what they said because it was likely the room they were in was bugged. He went again in 1990, with Uncle John, the year before Latvia became independent again.

After Walter arrived in England in 1947 he worked as a farm labourer, builder and miner. He'd work, work, work. People make assumptions about immigrants now and about how they are going to behave once they're here, but people don't know. If I knew what I know now when he was alive, I'd try to sit and talk with him. His eyes saw more than mine ever will.

I'm proud to be the grandson of a Latvian immigrant. He did alright out of it all by getting his head down and getting on with it. Making this programme made me realise why I'm happiest at work – it's the Latvian way. And it made me feel privileged to have a bit of Latvian blood in me.

26

CHAPTER 3

It was like swimming with a shark

AFTER LATVIA I was back on the trucks and putting in
a lot of miles on the pushbike, training for the Tour
Divide. I did a few days' filming around Lincolnshire
in early September for a programme about the Vulcan
bomber's last ever flight, only a month after the crash. It

involved going through the whole take-off procedure in the Vulcan. I was as sore as hell in that, but I didn't make a fuss in case someone said it wouldn't be a good idea for me to do it. I'd taken the day off work, so I wanted to get on with it. The seats weren't comfy, then there was the G-force, and even just getting up and down the stairs into the dead cramped cockpit was hard enough, the state I was in. It wasn't the worst pain in the world, but it wasn't good. It was worth it for the experience, though. We did exactly what a crew would do for a take-off, just stopping short of leaving the ground. I knocked the power off at the moment it wanted to leave the runway, then put it back on and the Vulcan wheelied. I also biked up to Inverness in January to the Strathpuffer endurance event to see how I'd cope on a bike and sleeping rough.

Then some more TV stuff was offered, when the BBC backed out of their Formula One deal three years early, because of budget cuts, and Channel 4 took over as the free channel to show the races. They asked if I wanted to be involved with some presenting. I didn't have to think about it for a minute, and told them, 'Thanks very much, but it's not for me.' I'm not a pundit. I don't want to be seen as someone telling someone else how to do their job. Some folk have made a job of talking about it, and that's fair enough, the job needs doing, but it's not for me. There might be another way of doing some TV bits on the technical side with the F1 in the future, but I had plenty on with the wall of death and the Tour Divide, so I didn't really need to be doing telly stuff when the season started.

A while later, Channel 4 wanted me to show my face at a press-night thing in London. It was a big party for the sponsors and advertisers, and all Channel 4's top bods were there. They'd rented out a fancy place in London to show clips of all the stuff that was going to be on the channel in 2016. Channel 4 and North One don't ask much of me on the PR side of things, because they know I don't like doing stuff like that, but both had asked me. I do bloody well out of the job, getting all sorts of opportunities, so I went.

While I was there Neil Duncanson, the boss of North One, said they had another idea. They wanted me to race a bike against a Formula One car. That was more up my street, and it could be filmed in two days, in the middle of February, before the F1 season, when things weren't too busy. I know plenty about Formula One, because I read *Race Engine Technology* magazine, and I was dead excited about it.

Over the next couple of weeks, more meat was put on the bones. It would be me versus David Coulthard. The hour-long programme would be filmed at Silverstone, the home of the British Grand Prix, and we'd have the place to ourselves for two days. The finished programme would be shown in the week before the start of the F1 season to help get people talking about the races being shown on Channel 4.

Coulthard would be driving a 2012 Red Bull RB8. Ideally, I wanted to use my Martek, the Pikes Peak bike, but I was too busy concentrating on building the wall of death bike to get it properly fettled, so Mark McCarville, the foreman from TAS (Temple Auto Salvage), the team I've raced for since 2011, brought over the BMW Superbike for me to ride. It gave the team a bit of coverage, so they were happy, and the closer the date came the more genuinely excited I was to get a chance to race against an F1 car.

I'd never met David Coulthard before the first morning. I was told later that he'd wanted to phone me up beforehand to suss me out, but the TV bods had put him off. I wouldn't really know what to say to him on the phone, but I got on with him from the off when we met at Silverstone. He's a nice, polite bloke. Articulate. Mick Moody deals with his brother, Duncan, because the Coulthards are in the haulage business. I got his brother's name from Moody and mentioned it to David, thinking it might be a bit of a conversation starter, but he explained that he knew nothing about the road haulage side of things. Disappointingly, he didn't even have a Class 1 truck licence, but we still had plenty to yarn about. He was interested in the TAS race bike, and I think he liked it that I was dead interested in the car. He knew everything about the set-up – spring rate, spring pressure, shims, brake biases – but he didn't know much about the recovery system the cars use now. I was never short of conversation with him.

The set-up of the two teams couldn't have been more different, and I heard it made for a good TV programme (but I never watched it). On the bike side were me and Mark. He'd set off at one in the morning to get the ferry over from Northern Ireland, with the bike and everything else we needed in the back of a high-top Vauxhall van. Coulthard had an 11-man pit crew, including one bloke they'd flown in from France especially to start the car.

The Red Bull RB8 is a 750 horsepower, 2.4 litre, V8 worth £5 million. It's the model of the car Sebastian Vettel won the 2012 Formula One title in. Coulthard, who has 13 Formula One race wins and 62 podiums to his name, had been involved in the development of the RB8 somewhere along the line.

When I saw the car versus bike challenges the TV lot had come up with, I didn't think the bike stood a chance of winning any of them. The first was a quarter-mile drag race the wrong way up Hangar Straight. There were some cones lined up to show where the start was and the finish line was a bridge over the track. I lined up and looked to my right, where it's not another bike, it's David Coulthard in a V8 F1 car! Bloody brilliant. I was on the Superbike spec BMW S1000RR. It has launch control, but I wasn't using it. I'm quicker setting off and controlling it manually, balancing the throttle, clutch and rear brake. With all the grip and power the F1 car's got, I thought Coulthard would smoke me. It was my first time on a superbike since breaking my back six months earlier, but I got off the line much quicker than the car. I was pressing hard on the back brake, to keep the front end down, and leading the car up to the halfway mark. Coulthard was coming fast and he just beat me, by three-tenths of a second. The terminal speeds were 159 mph for the car and 157 mph for the bike. Everyone was amazed how close it was.

The next challenge was braking from 100 mph. We did a lap of the track before coming on to the straight, where the car pulled up next to me. I set the speed and Coulthard matched me, because the bike has a speed read-out on its dash but the car doesn't. When we reached a line of cones we slammed on the anchors. The bike didn't stand a chance. If I braked too hard I'd lock the front wheel, risk skidding and losing the front, or I'd stoppie over the front of the bike. I'm braking with two fingers, feeling for the grip. Coulthard just pushed on the pedal as hard as he possibly could. They reckon F1 drivers push on the pedal with enough force to shift two full-grown men. The car could just lock its brakes and skid to a stop, and that's what it did. The car stopped from 100 mph in just over 50 metres. It took me 24 metres longer to come to a standstill, but there wasn't a lot of control going on in the car's lane – it was just locked up, going in a straight line, white smoke pouring off its fat tyres. We were quite even in the first bit of braking zone, until the car's tyres generated more heat and made it stick to the track surface even better and increase the rate it slowed. Coulthard ruined a pair of tyres beating me, though.

In between the challenges I had chance to quiz the mechanics to death. The car's steering wheel alone cost £27,000 and had a button on it that squirted a drink into the driver's gob. They don't even have to suck their own drinks. I had a go at changing a front wheel too, and on the second attempt I managed to do it in two seconds, about the same time an F1 mechanic is expected to do it in, but obviously I wasn't under the pressure of a pit lane halfway through a race. If I was ten years younger I'd jump at the chance of being an F1 mechanic. Coulthard had a go at changing the bike's back wheel and did it in less than a minute, longer than a TT mechanic would take, but I was still impressed.

Porsche has a Human Performance laboratory at Silverstone. They do physical assessments of folk and advise them on what they should do to improve their performance, from exercise to diet, and more specialist advice like dealing with competing in extreme heat. We went there and did a few physical challenges against each other. One involved pulling on this thing that measured hand grip while you lowered your right arm from horizontal to down by your side. My hand still had a load of metalwork in it from the crash a few months before, so I wasn't confident I'd win this one either. They reckon Aussie driver Mark Webber has a 65-kg grip. Coulthard's was 49 kg – mine was just under 36 kg.

Next was a test of reaction time, using a thing called a BATAK machine. It's a frame with red lights in the corners and middle, a bit like something you'd see in an arcade on Cleethorpes seafront. You smack the buttons when they light up, in a random order, and see how many you can put out in a minute. We were told that an F1 driver at the top of his game can turn off something like 60 in a minute, twice as many as the average person. Coulthard had done it before and scored 37. I was just behind with 35 on my first go. Another one I'd lost.

The car they were using, the RB8, was a few years old, for a couple of reasons. Driving a current car, even for a TV programme, would break the F1 testing ban. The other reason is that new F1 cars are too complicated to use for something like this. They have energy-recovery systems to make the most of the power the cars make. There are friction brakes on the wheels, like a regular car or motorbike, but they also have a retarder like on a truck. When you use the brakes on your car the forward motion is converted into heat that is just lost to the atmosphere. So instead of wasting the energy, they load the engine using a motor. An electric motor is bolted to the gearbox, and it works a bit like a starter motor but in reverse, so instead of trying to turn the motor forward, it is trying to turn it backwards, and acts like a brake. This motor works as both a motor and a generator to charge the battery when the car is braking, so when the car exits the corner it can use the energy it's just put in the battery to power itself and to give extra acceleration. Cars like the Toyota Prius have used similar ideas for years.

Because F1 fuel regulations are so tight the latest cars do another dead clever thing. When it goes into a corner a turbo car needs to vent the pressure in the plenum chamber – the pressurised airbox the engine breathes from – so you don't stall the turbo. But dumping the pressure you've built up into the atmosphere is also wasting energy. So, instead, the two halves of the turbo, the intake and exhaust, are split and linked with a shaft. The turbo can spin at 120,000 rpm, so the shaft runs through a gearbox with an output that drives a motor. Instead of dumping the plenum pressure, this motor connected to the shaft acts as a brake to slow down the turbo, and then reverts to being a motor to spin the turbo back up and reduce any turbo lag. It's dead clever. The saying is that racing improves the breed, and F1 is the pinnacle of racing technology.

Another two races were organised for day two.

The first was a slalom through nine cones spread in a straight line over 150 metres. It was a bit like a motorcycle CBT course. The car went first with its new front tyres, giving it more front grip. David explained that the throttle pedal movement is only summat like 50 mm, a couple of inches, and he was spinning the rear wheels to get the back end sliding to line up for the next gap between the cones. I was doing the timing with a stopwatch, stood right next to the finish line. There was a 30- or 40-metre gap between the last cone and the finish line, enough for him to gun it. He accelerated past where I was stood, two metres away, and I could feel the exhaust pulses in my chest. I stopped the clock at 12.87 seconds. He was happy with that, reckoning he had some good momentum. Then it was my go. I took it easy, dead smooth, swinging through the cones that were far enough apart to allow an F1 car through, which wasn't hard. I did it in less than ten seconds. We'd won one at last, but if I hadn't won that one I'd need to pack in.

The final test was a race around the Silverstone circuit. The TV lot looked at the F1 lap record and the motorbike lap record. The Superbike lap record at the time was 2:03. The F1 lap record was over 30 seconds quicker. So the car was quicker, no question, and a handicap race was the answer to keep things more interesting. It was worked out that a car should be able to do four laps in the time a bike could do three. Coulthard hadn't raced an F1 car for years and I was rusty, so it was a fair comparison.

Like in the drag race, I got off the line quicker and beat him into turn one, so I was happy with that, but he went around the outside of me and left at warp speed. He had to do 3.6 miles more than me, but he was doing 120 mph through Copse and I was nearly 40 mph slower, with my knee on the deck and the bike weaving and spinning on the cold track on the exit.

It was like swimming with a shark. I knew that if he did catch me I just had to keep doing what I was doing, not lift it up or be worried he was going to stick it underneath me. And he did catch me in the Farm section, with not much of my last lap to go. When he got me in his sights he couldn't take much out of me while we were both accelerating down the straights, but he made up so much time in the braking area. Obviously, there are no mirrors on a race bike, but I knew he was there, because I could hear him. The current F1 cars aren't as loud, but the car they used in the programme was the last of the V8s, and it was noisy – and actually a quicker car than the new one. He just came around the outside and it was game over. It was an honour to be involved with something like this.

We had Silverstone to ourselves, so after filming I did some laps, mucking about, and by the end of it I thought,

I'm bored of this now. It was another confirmation that I've had enough of racing motorbikes.

We didn't swap phone numbers – I'm not one for handing my number out and my phone is never turned on anyway – but if you're reading this, David, I'm still waiting for my invite down to Monaco.

CHAPTER 4

They needed to have faith in me

AROUND CHRISTMAS TIME the TV lot started talking about a new date for the wall of death attempt. The wall had been built and was sat idle, waiting for me in an aircraft hangar in Manby, Lincolnshire. March or April was mentioned – it had to be around then so that North

One TV's insurance company would be happy that my back injury wasn't going to be a problem. The idea, for those who didn't see it at the time, was to set the fastest-ever speed recorded on a wall of death. I was determined to do it on a bike I'd built myself and had started making parts for it on the milling machine in my shed.

We weren't messing. It was going to be the biggest wall of death ever, at least twice the size of any other in the world, and as the date got closer I was working flat out on the Rob North triple, my wall of death bike. Every spare minute I had was spent working on it. I felt that this was the biggest thing I'd done in motorcycling, and a big part of that was down to me building my own bike. Riding the wall itself wasn't what made it special, it was the whole thing combined – building the bike, the wall and the riding. Who is ever going to do that again? But all that would have to wait a while.

I went to see a back specialist after typing 'Spinal specialist Lincolnshire' into Google. It came up with Christopher Lee in Grimsby. I rang the receptionist, booked an appointment and went with Sharon to see him. He wasn't someone who specialised in treating motorbike racers, but he had seen enough. He was very thorough without being too cautious. Everyone around me had said I was doing too much, because I had gone back to work within two weeks of the accident, but he said if I was getting away with it, then that was alright.

After he'd looked at some X-rays he was happy enough with me doing whatever felt comfortable. He looked at what the surgeons had done in Belfast and said it was exactly how he'd have done it. Still, he wouldn't have a good idea about how long it would take me to get back to full fitness until I'd had a bit longer to heal. It could be six months, it could be a year, he explained, so I made an appointment to go back to him six weeks later. When I heard it might be a year I wasn't disappointed, it was just what it was going to be. You can't argue with the facts.

I also went to see Isla Scott, of Scott Physiotherapy on the Isle of Man, three times during the recovery. I'd drive over to Liverpool on a Wednesday, catch a cheap flight and fly back the same day. Isla would see to me until two o'clock, then I'd fly back at four – all done and dusted in the day.

I'd be there having four hours of massage treatment, to get the movement back in my neck and shoulders. I've known Isla for years and she's treated me for loads of knocks and strains, going back to the crash I had at the North West in 2008, so she knows what kind of movement I have when I'm fit and what she had to help me get back to.

During the first visit after the crash she didn't do much of what she calls manipulation, because the injury was all a bit fresh and still swollen, but she had the doctor's notes and was getting an idea of what had happened. I was telling people I was fine, that I'd just slept awkward, but I could hardly move my neck at first. I didn't have a lot of movement in my arms either. I was tight all over the place. She gave me a few exercises to do at home, but she was nervous of going hard at it. I did a load of the exercises and when I went back she gave me a load of new ones to do. Sharon went with me once, and there was an area that was hurting like buggery when Isla massaged it, because of a trapped nerve or summat, so Isla showed Sharon what to do so she could have a go at it at home. I only let Sharon do it once, but I think it cured it. After the third monthly visit to Isla I felt I was 100 per cent fit.

A big day in the whole wall of death job was when Ken Fox came to Manby to ride the big wall and prove it could be done. Ken was the programme's expert and the man who taught me how to ride on the wall. He is the son of a wall of death rider, and the Fox family have two walls of their own. Ken runs one of them with his youngest son, Alex, while his eldest, Luke, runs the other. They're at shows all over Britain and Europe from spring till Christmas.

Ken's test day on the big wall was 19 November. He was there with his missus, Julie; Ewan, Tom and Sarah came from North One; Paul and Curly from Krazy Horse brought their bike; and Sharon came with me. It had been worked out that a bike had to do a 4.5-second lap, at a minimum of 57 mph, to generate enough centrifugal force to stick to our big wall. Ken was the first and, until I was up to the job, only person to ride it. He rode a 2015 Indian Scout that had been built to his specification by Krazy Horse. The Indian made sense, as 1920s and 30s Indian Scouts are the traditional choice of bike to use on the wall of death. Other walls in the UK, Europe and the USA use the old American V-twins too. The Foxes run four of them, but use 1970s Honda CB200s, and that's what I was learning on.

Indian motorcycles are now made by a big American company called Polaris. Like all the companies that revive an old firm's brand name, they've used the famous model names of the original company, and the twenty-first-century Indian make a Chieftain and a Scout. The Scout is an 1130 cc, liquid-cooled V-twin cruiser. Krazy Horse of Bury St Edmunds, Suffolk, had been contacted to build a backup bike, in case the Rob North BSA triple I was busy building broke down. The attempt was going to be on live TV, so I couldn't be checking spark plugs if it played up.

Ken had visited Krazy Horse – they aren't far from him – and told them how he wanted it changing. He was well impressed that they'd done everything he'd asked. He wanted footboards (instead of footpegs), so he could move his feet back and forward, a shorter tank to allow the seat to move forward, and rigid forks and rear end, so no suspension at all.

On the smaller wall you're creating more centrifugal force at lower speeds, so you don't have to ride as quickly to stick to the wall, but the G-forces increase massively at much lower speeds than we wanted to attempt. Hugh Hunt, the doctor of mechanical engineering from Trinity College, Cambridge, who did the maths for the wall of death, says 80 mph on the small wall would exert 14 g, much more than a human could cope with.

It was always the plan, broken back or no broken back, that Ken was going to be the first man to test the wall. He had the most wall-riding experience and was the programme's expert. I was dead nervous watching him, even more nervous than I would be when it came to my chance to ride it. Everyone else was too, because only the maths said it was going to work – no one really knew. But I'd been into the wall weeks before and thought, Yeah, I can do this. Before that, I'd only seen the drawings and plans, and I was worried, thinking, When I see this with my own eyes will I be wondering what the hell have I said I'm going to do? Seeing it for the first time, even though it was massive, put my mind at rest.

When it came time to see how the bike would behave on the big wall, Ken put leathers and a helmet on. It would be the first time he had worn a motorcycle helmet on a wall of death. He looked like a fish out of water in all the borrowed kit. He did about ten laps of the track, the angled section at the bottom, came in and had a word with everyone about the time he was lapping it in. Then Ken went for it and proved to everyone it would work. The strangest thing was Ken admitting that this was the fastest he'd ever been on a motorbike. Not just on a wall of death, but in his life. A few people said he didn't look like he wanted to go back on the big wall, but he'd done his bit. Soon it would be my turn, but I had some more time on the little wall before I was ready for the big one.

I'd hardly been on a motorbike since the crash, and only ridden a road race bike at Silverstone against David Coulthard. I'd ridden a bit of flat track in October, just on the farm, but really I had about two-and-a-half days on a bike until I went back to the Foxes' in Cambridgeshire for two days of riding right at the beginning of March.

The Foxes' yard is out in the Cambridgeshire countryside. When it comes to their business the family are nearly self-sufficient. They have sheds and workshops in the yard as well as their homes. There are only a few jobs they don't do themselves, and I admire that. They maintain the trucks, mend the wall, do all their own paintwork – the family even built a new wall from scratch. They service the bikes and, when I was there, Luke and a couple of the other lads and lasses were converting a Transit van into a camper for one of the crew to sleep in when they're away at shows. When they've got a bit of spare time, Luke and his brother Alex modify cars: a Land Rover Discovery for off-roading and an old Mini with a Yamaha R1 1000 cc motorbike engine in it.

Up until recently, the whole family lived in the same yard, but Luke, Kerri and their little 'un had just moved out. Al_____ Abigail, in a static _____ park. Ken an_____ f like a section_____

The_____ as I got there _____ jumped out of _____ He had a gob_____ p to, so that v_____ t and he was _____ pe. The famil_____ alf-hour every now and then chasing and _____ the birds, so they weren't too surprised at Nige.

Tom and Sarah from North One TV were there, just keeping an eye on everything – they weren't filming me getting re-acclimatised to the wall. There were a couple of ambulance folk that the insurance company insisted had to be there. The whole insurance job around me and this wall of death was a carry-on, but it's just as well North One had it, as the cost of housing the wall in the hangar at Manby went through the roof because of the postponement. A couple of folk from national newspapers turned up at the yard for interviews.

It wasn't possible for me to just turn up after a few months and get straight on the wall – it was a bit tricky to get the hang of it again – but Ken was dead good, as he had been all along. He had me riding the track at the bottom, the angled transition between flat and vertical, a few times before attempting to get up on the wall. He's a brilliant teacher, really precise about what he wanted me to do: 'Right, ride the track, get up into second gear, then come back in, reset, have a cup of tea.' He wasn't assuming anything or expecting me to get straight back up there, and he wasn't putting any pressure on me. The opposite, really. He was always very measured about it all. Nothing was rushed, just take one step at a time again.

I was still getting dizzy. I was always dizzy if I rode long enough, but it gets better the more you do it. Before I turned up for the first day of practice, I thought I'd try to get away with doing only one day, but by the end of it I knew Ken expected me there the next day, so I drove the three hours home to do some work on the bike and set off early the next morning back to Cambridgeshire. Whichever way I went, I couldn't get the journey under three hours in either direction.

It was worth the drive because any spare time I had – nights, weekends, even an hour before setting off to work at half-five in the morning – from November onwards was spent building the Rob North BSA 750 triple I was going to use on the wall. I could have done with using the two days I was at Ken's improving the bike, but I knew it would be useful to spend time on the wall too.

Two weeks after my training down at Ken's yard it was my turn on the big wall. We were still 12 days away from the live TV programme, but it was a big day.

By now the Fox family had erected their own wall of death in one corner of the hangar at the disused Manby airbase, which was nearly full to bursting with the big wall. Ambulance and fire crews were there, as well as the TV bods, Krazy Horse folk, a load of the Fox Troupe's extended family and my dad.

I turned up in the van with Sharon and Nige, and the Rob North BSA (let's just call it the triple to save time) in the back. It wasn't totally finished, but the TV bods wanted to see it. They had expected me to finish the bike and test it on an airfield or summat weeks before, but they should have read *When You Dead, You Dead*. If they had, they'd have seen: 'Even though I'd really like to have it finished and sat in the shed ready and waiting to go, that's not going to happen. It'll become a priority when it becomes a priority.'

And that's what happened. I wanted to make a load of parts for it myself, not sub them out or buy them in.

But that meant I had to learn how to make them too. My dad came over to mine to work with me on it for four or five Sundays on the trot towards the end of the job.

To build the triple I had to learn CNC machining. I only went on the course that would teach me enough to make the bits to build the bike on 23 December, at OneCNC in Dudley. They make a CAD (computer aided design) system that works with my XYZ milling machine. I was a bit stuck so they squeezed me in, but it meant I was the only person on the course. I'd had the OneCNC system on my laptop for a year, and I'd taken it to New Zealand over Christmas 2014, because I'd been told to try to learn it a bit myself so I knew what they were on about when I took the free classroom course that came with the system. I didn't know any CAD beforehand, and I didn't really need it until I got into building this bike. I struggled on without it, using my milling machine, but not to anything like its potential.

A CAD program like SolidWorks is easier for drawing parts and altering the drawings, but when it comes to making toolpaths for the milling machine to follow, it's not as easy as OneCNC's system. I thought I could just draw what I wanted and send it to the machine, and it would make the part and I'd be away. But it doesn't. The machine doesn't understand the picture. It only understands numbers, so you have to convert the drawing into numbers, but that's not as easy as it sounds.

After the course there was still something I couldn't work out, so Sharon rang up XYZ, who make the CNC milling machine. They realised that it was to do with a certain code that was defaulting to imperial, not metric measurements.

Now my head was filled with approach distances, tool radii, selecting boundaries, work offsets, feeds and speed in millimetres per minute. It all makes my brain hurt, but I like it. Sometimes I think I've got it all right, but I've missed a number and the tool flies into the job at 100 mph and knackers it, so I've had to learn.

It probably took me six hours to draw the top yoke and get it ready for machining, but then it would take the CNC milling machine 15 hours to cut it. I'd set it going at ten at night and leave it cutting, and I'd wake up at four, worried, and have to go downstairs to check it.

It would have been dead easy to find a place in Grimsby to do the machining, but whatever happened I knew I had to suss it and do it myself. It was important to me. I only buggered one big bit up, the bottom yoke. But now I can draw a part and program a CNC machine, which gives me a lot of satisfaction.

Then the CNC milling machine's motor shit itself, so I'm now a CNC machine fitter too. I wasn't going to pay some bugger to come out and fix it.

So, the triple wasn't quite finished, but we were nearly two weeks from the live broadcast on Easter Monday. It

was always the plan that I was going to ride the Krazy
Horse Indian on this test, and that was all ready and
looking bloody nice. After all, Ken had proved it worked
at 57 mph. The TV bods said they wanted to see my
bike running, but it wouldn't start. Then it pissed oil all
over the car park. It wasn't the best first impression, I'll
admit that, but they needed to have faith in me. I knew it
wasn't ready. I knew I was cutting it fine, but the TV lot
started really panicking. No one was saying a thing to
me, but they were on to Andy Spellman, my agent, and I
was hearing it from him. They were shitting themselves,
but none of them would say it to my face and I don't
know why.

My bike looked the same as it does now, and how it
looked on telly, except it didn't have a seat, just some
padding taped on. Ken wasn't impressed. He didn't like
the clutch and primary drive being all open. I'd made it
clear from the start that my triple was going to be the
number one bike and the Krazy Horse Indian Scout was
the backup. After the TV lot saw my bike they didn't
want me to use it. They had seen what a good job Krazy
Horse had done, so they asked them to build another
Indian Scout, just the same. So now the backup bike had
a backup bike.

All this happened before I even got my leathers on to
attempt my first ride on the wall. I don't know if the
distraction of the triple puking its oil up had anything

to do with it, but I wasn't feeling that nervous. I'd seen it done, I'd trained on the small wall and I know how to ride a motorbike. Let's have it, I thought, as I walked into the wall of death.

After the bike had a couple of minutes to warm up, Curly, the mechanic from Krazy Horse, took the tyre warmers off and I climbed on. I rode the track, slowly at first, then came in for a word from Ken. Then I rode the track until I was going at a speed where the bike wanted to go on to the wall, and I was forcing it to stay on the track. I stopped again, then went out, up to speed and on to the wall for a few laps.

I was a bit wild at first, bouncing off the track, up the top, down the bottom. I felt a bit out of control. Ken was dead calm, but he was telling me I didn't need to be going that fast to start with. He never once said I was going too slow, and he was right – back off and build up slowly. Like Ken had warned me, a tiny movement made a huge difference on the big wall. I had to be more precise than I was on the small one.

I came in for a breather and a reset. I also let Curly check the bike over before I went out for more of the same. Once I'd reset myself and got the gist of it, I was alright. What I had underestimated was the G-force, even at the low speeds. I might have been in the early 60s, way off the 80-mph target, but I was already really feeling the effect of 3.5 g. I'd done all the G-force training, going up in the stunt plane with pilot Mark Greenfield, and had a day of training with the RAF fighter pilots, but I thought it was all a bit of TV bullshit to make something to show on telly. It wasn't. I was the limiting factor of it all.

While I didn't feel nervous, a heart-rate monitor I wore clocked me at 190 bpm. I thought the only way for me to get my heart rate that high was to go like hell on a pushbike, so it must have been adrenaline.

That first afternoon on the big wall made it clear that the riding position of the modified Indian, even though it was an improvement over the standard riding position, wasn't perfect. For a road bike it would be spot on, but I felt the bars were still too far from the seat. When I got up enough speed to get on the wall, about 60 mph, I was already feeling 3 to 4 g, and, because of the angle of my body, the extra G-force was pushing my chest and head down towards the top of the petrol tank. It was as if a big hand was pressing the centre of my back. It was nothing to do with the back injury – I was totally over that. It was all down to the body position. Being pushed down like that made it hard for me to see where I was going.

Ken Fox didn't agree that there was anything wrong with the Scout. His view was, 'It's spot on. Just ride it.' And at the lower wall speed of 57 mph it was, but go faster than that and you're sat in the wrong place. Ken has a motorbike and he rides it, pissing with the cock he's got. I'm used to racing bikes, and if something doesn't feel right I change it. I change this, change that, change everything I can to improve it. In racing you tailor everything to make it easier to do what you want. I applied my road-racing methods to the wall of death bike, saying to Krazy Horse, 'I don't like this, can you change it?'

After that first day on the big wall Dad said, 'I'd use the Indian. I wouldn't ride the triple,' even though he'd been working hard on it with me. Curly had done a good job on the Indian and he had the same double-check work ethic of a good TT mechanic, that wasn't a doubt. But that wasn't the point. I didn't need a boot up the arse to get the triple finished, but it just confirmed that I was definitely riding the triple, especially if my dad thought that.

CHAPTER 5

I was 100 metres from the work gates when ...

I HAD A bad run with the Transit vans, starting not long after I broke my back at the Ulster Grand Prix in August 2015. It was one thing after another, with the first coming on the way to work one morning. I'd had the use of Transits for years, but they'd always been work vans, either my dad's or Moody's, none with my name on the logbook. But FT13 AFK, a black Transit Custom, was mine. Before that I'd owned Vauxhall Astravans and a Volkswagen Transporter, but Transits were the vans I liked the most.

I was still getting over my back injury, so I was only biking into work a couple of days a week and driving the rest of it while I built up my fitness. It was September, earlyish in the morning, and the autumn sun was dead low, just rising, when I turned into the industrial estate. I was 100 metres from the work gates when I drove into the back of a parked car transporter. It was a hell of a shock. The impact ripped the nearside of the van out, demolishing the headlight, pulling the suspension wishbone off and the driveshaft out, and buckling the floor up. I'd only just turned the corner, so I wasn't going fast, maybe 20 mph, but I hit 15 tons of lorry that wasn't about to move and bounced off the transporter on to the other side of the road. I'd been there about a minute, still trying to work out how I'd managed to crash into a parked truck, when another van came around the corner and did exactly the same thing.

The transporter was parked opposite a junction, where it shouldn't really have been, but it was my fault. He wasn't moving, and I'd driven straight into him because I was blinded by the sun.

The police turned up, heard what happened and were

accusing me, and the other bloke who'd crashed, of driving without due care and attention. What could I say to that? I'd just driven into a stationary truck. Luckily, matey boy who'd crashed after me had an onboard video camera in the cab of his van, and it showed you could not see a thing, so the police became a bit more understanding. Still, it didn't change the fact that my van was a write-off. I couldn't be without a van, so the same day I bought one from a local dealer who owed me a favour and got a good deal on a plain white Transit, with a poverty spec.

I ended up buying the wreck from the insurance company too. It had been labelled a Category B write-off by the insurance assessors, which meant there were strict rules saying it couldn't be used on the road again. I didn't know what I was going to do with it, but I'd owned it from new and driven it carefully – it had just clocked 95,000 on the original brake discs and pads – so I reckoned it was too good to scrap. I managed to buy the wreck back for £900 and got paid out decent insurance money too, so it could've been worse.

The next Transit disaster, or near disaster, happened in December, when I went to my favourite butty van, Gina and Nicky's, close to work. I'd driven up to get something to eat and parked all of 40 metres from the butty van. I climbed out and walked halfway to it when I remembered I'd left all my change in my van and walked back to get it. Then, when I opened the Transit door, I realised I had the money in my pocket after all. I emptied everything out of my overalls on to the front seat, picked out the loose change, left the work and van keys on the front seat, closed the door and walked back to the butty van.

I got my grub, turned around and said, to no one in particular, 'Where's me van gone?' A woman in the queue for her own dinner said someone had just climbed out of a car, jumped in the van and driven off. Keen fucker! There was no sight of it, and it was obvious it wasn't just Moody or Belty playing a trick on me. It had been nicked. I ran back to work thinking, How am I going to tell Moody this?

I got into the office, rang the coppers and told them exactly what happened. I knew that if the van was gone for good it would be coming out of my pocket. The insurance wouldn't cover it because I'd left the keys in it. All that was going through my mind was, Shit, bugger, bastard! Then, half an hour later, the phone rang. It was the police, telling me they'd found the van. It turned out the thieves had driven it off the industrial estate, round the corner and parked on a posh street, or as posh as it gets in Grimsby, locked it up and left it. The police reckoned the thieves would leave it there until the dust settled then go back for it after dark. My work keys were still on the seat, so I got away quite lightly. I just had to have new locks put in the van. That cost £300, but it was obviously loads better than buying a new van and having all the security at Moody's changed. Another narrow escape.

The van that was nicked and missing for all of half an hour, thanks to the Grimsby police, was a work Transit, but I had the white poverty spec van, and then a grey Transit L2 H2 turned up from Ford as part of a deal I'd done with their TrustFord division, opening the new Transit plant at Dagenham, in January.

On that day I met 15 of TrustFord's apprentices, and we had a bit of banter. TrustFord is the company's UK dealer network, and I was interviewed by their apprentice of the year, Ben Dodds. It sounds like Ford has got a good set-up for their apprentices. The courses they run teach them the ins and outs of the trade. When I did my apprenticeship, working on Volvo trucks for John Hebb, I did day release at a good college with good teachers, but we'd work on old knackers that didn't have much relevance to what we were actually dealing with at Hebb. The TrustFord lads are learning about modern technology on the latest vans and cars.

Dagenham is massive, with hundreds of brand new Transits parked on-site. I knew the vans were made in Turkey, but I didn't know the engines were all built in Dagenham, then shipped out to Turkey, fitted into Transits they've assembled and then shipped back to England. It doesn't sound very efficient, but that's what happens.

When the grey Transit L2 H2 (that's the medium wheelbase, medium height option) turned up, I ended up giving the white van to my big sister Sal.

About the same time, Warren Scott, the owner of Rye House speedway track, down in Hertfordshire, contacted me and Matt Layt about riding KTM 450s as part of a dirt-track team for him. Matt is a mate from my days riding British Superbikes and he's got into dirt track. At the back end of January, I was over in West Yorkshire picking the KTM up in my two-week-old grey Transit when someone ploughed into the side of it at a junction. I wasn't best pleased. I was upset for months when someone put a ding in the door of FT13 AFK after opening a door on it in a car park, but this was something else. Three Transits: one written off, one stolen and recovered, and another stoved-in, in less than five months. It's a good job I'm insured.

CHAPTER 6

80.8 mph riding blind

ONE WEEK BEFORE the live attempt, I started on more intensive training on the big wall while I continued to work on the Rob North triple. The TV lot were still panicking about me not being ready, but they were under more pressure than usual, because the show was going to be live. For me, though, from now on it was all about increasing my speed and finding out how much G-force I could deal with.

I got Cammy on board to be the triple's mechanic, checking it after every run and keeping it fettled, and I'm dead glad I did. He had been a mechanic for me at the TT and came to Pikes Peak with me. He came down on Monday, the first day of the week of practice, while I was at work. He went to my house and met Sharon, and drove to Manby with the triple in the van. It was nearly ready, but the gearbox was still shit. I left work that day about dinnertime for the 25-mile cycle ride to Manby. I cycled there on a few of the practice days so I could keep up my preparation for the Tour Divide, because I had to build up to 300 miles a week. I could see the hangar for miles – all the trucks, camper vans, satellite dishes – and I thought, That's all for me, that is.

The triple was finished to a state I was dead happy with, and the TV bods said, 'OK, you've got it done,' but I know they didn't trust me. They love the idea that I'm a truck mechanic who does a bit of bike building and TV stuff, but really they think I'm a TV wanker. They don't believe I build bikes. They weren't happy to let me ride it on the wall until they had an independent engineer assess it and say it's safe to ride. They asked me who I knew who could do that, and the first person I thought of was Mark Walker, who was one half of Martek, the folk who originally built my Pikes Peak bike. And he was handy, because he lived not far away. I gave the TV lot his number and they quickly arranged for him to come the next day.

Mark did his assessment of the bike at the Manby hangar. He had a good look over it and said, 'Yeah, spot on, but I've got to say something, so I'll advise that you should have a cover on the clutch.' He even liked that the clutch was open, but I knew he had to be seen to be doing something. I'm not sure what they thought this clutch was going to do. It makes sense to have the primary drive covered on a road racer, where it could come into contact with another rider, but this bike was built for the wall of death, with only me on it, and no other bikes or folk around.

After Mark had given it the 'official' all-clear, except for the clutch cover, I said, 'I'm here, I may as well have a go on the wall now that everyone is happy with the triple.' Tom, the producer and project manager, and Ewan, the director, said I could ride it on the track, but not the wall. So I set off on the triple round the track. It felt alright, so I gave it a bit more throttle and went on the wall. They went off their tits: 'Insurance! We said just go on the track!' I explained that it was the bike, not me – it wanted to go on the wall. Nothing to do with me. From then on the bike never missed a beat or dripped a drop of oil.

The gearbox selector mechanism was shit, though. You can see why the British bike industry went bust.

It had a Heath Robinson system to do a really simple job. Me and my dad had been filing and fettling and fucking about and it still wasn't any good, so my dad got in contact with Richard Peckett, who made famous race frames and bikes with a partner under the name P&M. He had a brand new part for the gearbox that we needed. We fitted the new selector arm and straight away it was perfect. I made the smallest clutch cover you could imagine, just to keep everyone happy, and that was it. I'd done it on time. Everything I'd done was right, but it had been a non-stop rush since November and there were some little finishing jobs I'd have liked to have done, so Cammy got on with them. He drilled and lockwired all the things he thought needed it.

I did wonder if the TV lot would say I had to ride the Indian and nothing else. If they could argue that I had to use the Indian for good, solid reasons, I'd have said, 'Alright, then,' and I'd have ridden the Indian. But if it was because I felt they didn't trust my work on the triple I'd have told them they'd best get someone else to ride the wall. I know what I'm talking about – I've been building bikes since I was a kid and I'm a good mechanic. I wasn't about to do something this dangerous on a bike I didn't have faith in, but I know the insurance was probably a big part of it too.

There's usually the easy option and the shitty, wanky option, and I usually choose the shitty, wanky one. Like when I did Pikes Peak. Taking the TAS BMW Superbike would've been the easy route, and I'm not being a big head but I'd have won the race outright on it. Instead, I built the Martek turbo that was in a thousand bits and took that.

Riding the Indian on the wall of death would have been the easy route. Krazy Horse did a brilliant job and we could've concentrated on one bike and got it loads better. By now, we had put rear suspension back on the Indian, fitting fancy K-Tech twin shocks. When they're built for a road bike they have 250 psi of pressure in them. For the wall they had 550 psi, and they were still bottoming out. They were great until they bottomed out, but when they did it made it worse, because the back end had squatted and that altered the front geometry, effectively kicking the forks out. K-Tech would have altered the shocks for me and they were dead keen to help with my triple bike too, but I ended up using Hagon shocks because I wanted to do my own thing. Hagon make shocks for Rob North frames, so I asked if they could do something similar, but make them as stiff as they could with as short a distance of travel as they could, and they made me these dead simple shocks.

Krazy Horse had already spent £7,000 on machining a few parts for the Indian Scout: the footboard assembly and the solid struts that replaced the rear shocks. It looked brilliant and it never missed a beat, but I needed to be sat more upright. Either the bars needed to come back to me or the seat needed to move closer to the bars. In the end, they did a bit of both. Then, after another practice, they moved the bars back again. None of this was easy. They cut and shortened the petrol tank and had it repainted, but it was such a neat job, you'd never know. They had lovely new bar clamps machined, which moved the bars right back.

With both bikes sorted I could just concentrate on the riding and going 80 mph on the biggest-ever wall of death. In the mid- to late-60s it was already getting difficult to hold my body in a good riding position, and that wasn't much quicker than the lowest speed you can get on the wall. Late-60s on is when I really had to tense up and hold my breath, pushing all my muscles, like I was taught by the fighter pilots. Then, as I went faster, my vision would go.

There was a green line, top to bottom of the wall – the start and finish line, if you like – and a red line around the wall to let me know where I was in relation to the top and bottom. The lap was timed from the green line, so I'd cross it, but wait until I had done half a lap before I wound on the throttle. I knew that by the time I was back to the green line I'd be up to speed for a flying lap. The problem was that, by the time I got back to the green line, after only half a lap of hard acceleration, I could hardly see anything – my vision had pretty much gone because I was greying out. I was still conscious, but the blood ran out of my eyes. I'd tense everything – stomach, legs – and blow inside of my closed mouth to puff my cheeks. It's hard to explain, but my vision gradually goes like a sparkly, untuned telly. Halfway through the flying lap I can see even less, then I'm blind for another half a lap, just guessing when I'm over the green line and I can back off. Then, my vision comes back. When I knock off the throttle, I don't do anything drastic. I just wait for my vision to return so I can spot the red line. It doesn't come back instantly, but very quickly.

I wasn't thinking too hard about suddenly passing out under the G-force, but I knew what could happen if I did. The best case would be to slump forward and close the throttle. If I did that, I might regain consciousness and, with the G-force decreased, be able to steer the bike to a stop. If I didn't regain consciousness in time, but I had let off the throttle, the bike would slow down, dip towards the track at the bottom and I'd fall off. The worst-case scenario was falling unconscious, somehow winding on the throttle and going out of the top of the wall. There was a steel cable, held by heavy brackets around the top, to stop the bike going into the crowd. If I went out of the top I'd be short of an arm or leg at the very best.

I felt I put in a quick lap on Thursday night. Sharon and Cammy both thought it was a fast one, and the speed of it frazzled my brain. It felt like early 80s. I was driving home, while Cammy and Sharon were chatting, but I was gone. When we passed the pub at the bottom of my road I asked, 'Shall we go for a pint?' I'm not a drinker, but Cammy likes a pint, so I pulled straight into the car park. I didn't even drive the 200 yards to the house. I had a pint of Guinness and I fancied another while we talked about all sorts, and two pints later I felt alright.

I could always go quicker on the triple, right from day one. I'm sure it was because of the riding position. Perhaps some of the crew thought I was trying harder to go faster on my bike, because I'd built it and was stubborn about wanting to use it, but it wasn't like that. I just always felt more comfortable on the triple.

The only thing I'd change about it was the rear suspension. It has about 30 mm of movement, but I'd make it stiffer. It was spot on to about 60-odd mph, then it got a bit rough. It has 15 mm of travel and 15 mm of rubber bump stop that compresses as the G-force increases. Then it bottoms out and there's no more suspension. So, if I was doing it all again, I'd make it stiffer so it didn't move through the first 15 mm of suspension quite so easily.

Months and months before, I would spend the night in the shed with Sharon and cable tie her legs in different places and move her hands in different places to try to get the riding position like I thought it should be. That was before I had any wheels in the bike. Then I would go to bed thinking about it. We tried all kinds of handlebars, but I couldn't find any that were dead right until I had a word with my uncle Rodders (who isn't really my uncle), and he brought some round that I ended up using.

Those few days of practice were my idea of the perfect week. I had a bit of pressure on at work, because a job had to be out, and I was biking to work, then biking to Manby – no filming, just riding. Sharon and Cammy there, the dog's there, I'm riding Ken's wall as well. Ken asked me if I was doing all this just so I could ride the big wall or because I wanted to be a wall rider. I said I wanted to be a wall of death rider and do some shows with him. Ken was becoming more confident with me, and he told me that before the end of it all we'd both ride on his wall together. And we did, but it was hairy.

I set off around the small wall on a Honda 200, and Ken was half the wall behind me on another Honda. He'd told me that I would go to the top so he could go underneath me. He overtook me and then pulled in front of me, and that was my signal to move to the bottom of the wall and pass him, while he rode around the top. I got a bit lost, forgetting what I was supposed to be doing, but he'd already accounted for that, because he said that if anything went adrift he'd come in and get out of the way to let me pull in. When Ken talks, don't speak, listen.

I think the challenge of riding the big wall at 80 mph was far harder than riding at 180 mph down Bray Hill at the TT. At wall speeds in the low 60s, it was a case of, Yeah? What's the problem, officer? I could move about, even ride one-handed, like Ken had suggested. Go late 60s, however, and it suddenly got very difficult.

I only ride for selfish reasons, because I want to ride. Ken is a showman – he's at the opposite end of the scale. When I was practising on the little wall, Ken said, 'Right, you can put your hand out now.' I thought, Why would I want to do that? But I did and it gave me assurance that I knew what I was doing. It became a good gauge to see if I was confident enough. It was only for me, not putting on a show. I wasn't giving a flick of the wrist like the full-time riders would, playing to the crowd. I'd just put my arm out like I was on a pushbike and doing a lazy signal to show car drivers I was turning left, nothing fancy.

I would only take my hand off on the big wall at lower speeds. Your hand's heavy, its increased weight caused by the G-force. If I put my hand on the bar like I normally would, just releasing the muscle pressure and letting it drop on the bar, it could unsettle the bike and send me into a wobble, so I had to be dead careful and controlled.

Ken had told me not to change gear on the wall, because if I hit a false neutral I'd be in trouble, but I was doing it anyway when I'd built my confidence up. He didn't like me doing it and, while changing gear on the wall, I broke the gear linkage on the Indian because I was pressing so hard on it with all the extra G-force. It was the only breakage we had to deal with.

Once I'd got up to a certain speed on the wall, no one had done more relevant experience than me of this kind of riding. At this point it was more important what Curly and Cammy, the two blokes looking after the bikes, were saying. As long as the bikes were alright I was on my own. Ken had got me to this stage, but now it was into the unknown.

I thought Ken, Luke and Alex would all be begging to go on the big wall and show how fast they could go, but none of them did. I don't know if they didn't fancy it or if they were doing the professional thing and staying out of the way of the TV bods, but none of them asked me if they could have a go and I was a bit surprised about that. It was a potentially dangerous job, though, and if it did go wrong it could be a bomb scene.

Everything was going smoothly until Friday. Almost as soon as I got on the wall I was blacking out – not unconscious, just blind. I didn't crash, because when it happened I knew I had to back off the throttle and my vision would come back. I wondered if it was because I hadn't biked in, or was it because I'd had two pints the night before?

I rode on the Saturday and took my turbo trainer. I hadn't had any alcohol and drank loads of water, so I was well hydrated, and I was still the same. I couldn't even reach 70 mph without blacking out. I kept going on the wall, then coming off it. Going on and doing some laps, then coming back down, putting my body through it, and it didn't make any difference. I couldn't understand what was happening.

That afternoon I did a timed 54-mph lap. The added friction of the tyres must have kept the whole lot up as well, meaning I didn't have to do the theoretical 57 mph that had been worked out on paper.

On Sunday, the day before the TV show, I didn't try to set a high speed and took it real steady. It was like the Wednesday night of practice before the Senior TT – just get your lap in, no heroics. I still didn't know if I'd black out at 70 mph or if I could set a fast time.

On the day of the TV show, I walked the dog in the morning and visited my gran, Double-Decker Lil, who I hadn't seen for a month because I'd spent every spare minute building the triple. Near my gran's, Nige got in a bit of bother and cut his leg. I reckon he got shot by the pheasants he'd been chasing. I was on my pushbike with him and sweating my tits off getting my heart rate right up, hoping that would help the blacking-out problem. I went with Sharon to the wall at about dinnertime.

There's normally half-a-dozen people there at the most when I'm filming. Someone told me there was a crew of 100 involved in this show. Lighting folks, directors, fitters, security, ambulance, cameras, catering ... over an Easter weekend, too. Fill your boots, lads. Surprisingly, it was all water off a duck's back to me. I was just riding my bike and, even writing this, I still haven't really taken in that it was all for me. I never felt any pressure.

Before the live broadcast we did what was pretty much a full rehearsal of the hour-and-a-half programme. It was good, because they didn't use me for all of it. So, when it came to live transmission, I was in it a lot more and not repeating what I'd been asked to rehearse. They knew if I was asked the same questions in the live programme that I was in rehearsal I'd lose interest. When I'm being filmed I'm not thinking about what I should say, I just answer the questions. I can play the game, I've been doing it long enough, but I still thought they were brave doing it live, because I know I can ramble on when I'm asked something. They have a job editing me sometimes, and, obviously, they couldn't do that with this.

By now I knew both bikes were up to the job, but riding any bike, especially the triple, really was a trip into the unknown. The Indian was fuel-injected, but the much older BSA triple engine had Keihin 34 mm carbs, which I wasn't sure would be able to deal with the 6 or 7 g that they might be forced to work under. I was worried that the plastic float in the bottom of the carb – which, as you might have guessed, floats on the fuel in the floatbowl – might sink through the fuel and flood the carb. I also didn't know if the fuel coming up the emulsion tube would have to fight against the G-force, and I wondered if that was going to be a problem. The G-force overpowers blood pressure – that's what causes people to black out – so it seemed possible it would cause a problem for the engine too.

I spoke to Matt Markstaller, who is the man who built the Triumph streamliner that I plan to ride at Bonneville for another record later in the year, and he put some doubt in my mind. He thought about it and rang me back saying it would cause a problem, because the float at 7 g is seven times heavier than it is just sat on the road, so he reckoned that even though the fuel would be seven times heavier too, it isn't seven times more dense.

A month or two before the record attempt I spoke to the lads at Wirth Research in Bicester, who do Formula One simulations and computational fluid dynamics for some of the top teams. I had met the lads at Wirth before, when they did some simulations of the downforce of a spoiler for a Transit van (but that's another story). I gave them the numbers and sizes and they chewed it over. Wirth thought there might be an effect, but not a problem with the fuel coming up the emulsion tube and into the airstream, before it's sucked down the inlet manifold towards the head and intake valves.

Finally, I spoke to Dr Hugh Hunt, the man who worked out the numbers behind the wall of death itself.

This was on the afternoon of the attempt, so a bit late, but by now I was sure, in my own head, that there was no problem. I should have spoken to him from the start, because he came straight out and explained that none of that mattered because of Archimedes' principle. I could balance a washing-up bowl of water on the petrol tank and put an apple in it, then ride the wall of death, and the apple wouldn't sink or float higher in the water. It would stay the same, because the water the apple displaces weighs the same as the apple and that's a constant. 'Oh yeah,' I said, 'I didn't think of it like that.' I should've spoken to Hugh six months ago.

Steve Jones had been chosen as the live show's presenter. Davina McCall had been lined up for the original date that was postponed, but I wasn't bothered who did it really. I'd met Steve at Silverstone a month before, when I was filming with David Coulthard. I think Steve was eyeing the job up because he's doing some F1 stuff with Channel 4. From the off I had him down as a TV wanker because he had sunglasses on, even though it was overcast, but it wasn't a problem. If you don't remember, a TV wanker isn't a wanker, just a TV wanker. The ones I work with joke about it. They get it – they don't take offence. Steve was very professional, thinking hard about what he was doing. I liked him.

In the rehearsal I had a good go on the wall, just to be sure I wasn't going to black out, and I did a recorded

80.8 mph, riding blind, just pointing and not making any movements so I stayed as close to the line as I could. Even though all the timing was official, you have to inform the Guinness record people before you start that you are going to attempt a world record. The woman from the Guinness was stuck on a train, so it isn't official, but I know I did over 80. That's all that matters.

After the rehearsal I had a few hours to hang about, before the live show. The whole day was dead relaxed and there was always someone interesting to talk to: Sharon, Ken, Curly, Cammy, my dad, my good mates Jonty and Ruth came, Isla Scott, Hugh Hunt, and my dog, Nige, was there. Coulthard flew in from Monaco to Humberside International Airport (I did wonder how many times that journey had been made before). I could make a brew when I wanted and there was no pressure. It wasn't like I was the epicentre. I felt like a small cog in a machine, and the people who were there were either working or knew me well enough that they could see me the following week.

My mum and sisters were there, too. My little sister does all that tweeting shit. I didn't want her to be taking photos and tweeting them, but she did anyway and it annoyed me. My brother Stu was racing at Donington, and he didn't make it back in time.

Part of the programme was to have the former world BMX champion and British Olympic rider Shanaze

Reade set a record for cycling speed on Ken's wall of death. She'd been there for a few days, being taught by the Foxes and riding with Alex Fox a lot. I liked her, and she was another one who was dead straight-talking. She asked if I'd ever been for a bike-fit, where someone tells you how you're supposed to sit on your bike for the optimum power output, because she didn't like how I sat on mine. I had, Brian Rourke did one for me, but I do enough miles to know what I like and what I don't like, so I changed it all back. The seat's at the wrong angle, for most people at least, and the pedals are wrong. She knows what she's on about, but I have my seat like that to stop my bollocks going numb.

Then, it all started. While the programme was live, there were pre-recorded sections slotted in: the first time I went on Ken's wall, when I went up in the stunt plane and when I met Hugh Hunt to talk about the science behind it all. There was a fifteen-minute delay on the broadcast, so what people were watching on their tellies at two minutes past seven had actually happened fifteen minutes earlier. The reason for this was that there was a fair chance it could all go pear-shaped, and no one wants to see a lorry mechanic plough into his family and friends live on TV. Or not many do, anyway.

The only time it felt like this was a really big thing was when I walked out into the middle of the wall for Steve Jones to introduce the programme and saw all the folk who had been invited on the viewing platform. I thought, Hell, that's a lot of people. I had a massive smile on my face, because I thought Steve Jones was cool and he did a right good job.

Shanaze was up first, her record attempt was quite early in the programme. She and Alex Fox had been having a bit of friendly rivalry about the speeds during practice. Alex actually put in a faster unofficial speed, but Shanaze set the official record at 26.8 mph during the live programme.

I had new black Dainese leathers with 'Kirmo' written on the front. The TV lot had rung Spellman, my agent, to ask what Kirmo meant, because I wasn't allowed to show 'undue prominence' of sponsors' logos. Kirmo is Kirmington, the village I grew up in and the centre of the universe, but I joked on TV that it was my dog Nige's Cayman Islands-based finance company. I don't know if anyone got that when I said it on telly, but I thought it was funny.

Then it was time to ride. First I went out on the Indian and set the record at 70.33 mph, beating the 60-mph limit that would get the attempt an official Guinness record, and then I had a go on the triple. I was over the moon that I'd done 80 mph in practice, but I couldn't quite do it again on TV.

I came in and was told I'd done 78.15 mph. I asked if I could have another go, but they'd run out of time and it didn't happen. I'd pushed my luck. I wasn't thinking, Give me another hour on this thing. I was never going to do 90 mph. I might have done 85, but it was all guesswork, because I was riding around blind. I'm not sat here thinking anyone has denied me a chance. I have no regrets, because you can't see what I could see, which was fuck all. I bet I shut off a fraction before the green line on the live telly attempt. I had proved I'm not a TV wanker, too.

I was dead pleased with how it all went, but I was most pleased for the Channel 4 and North One lot: Neil Duncanson, Ewan, Tom and the rest. It had been a way of life for them for a month. They'd thought about everything, and the hard work and effort they put in impressed me and stuck with me more than the experience of riding the wall at 80 mph. It was a long programme for four or five minutes of riding, but I didn't hear anything negative about it.

There was a big after-show party at the hotel the TV lot were all staying at, but Sharon, Cammy and his missus, Hannah, loaded the van up with me, and we got back to my house at about ten, unloaded the van, had a beer and went to bed because I had to be at work the next morning. There was no high-fiving or whooping. I gave Cammy the Guinness certificate. I'm not ungrateful, but it doesn't mean anything to me. Never say never, but I'd be surprised if this record is ever broken.

I got into work the next morning, but Moody wasn't there. He turned up late and explained that his missus had an epileptic fit in the audience and got taken away in an ambulance. He said, 'That was embarrassing, wasn't it? I missed the best bit.' Dry as you like. It was all too much for Belty, our valeter at the truck yard, and he didn't turn up till Wednesday.

I'm glad I managed to achieve what I set out to do, but even in the van on the way home on Easter Monday I was saying to Sharon, 'What's the next thing?'

CHAPTER 7

I'd only slept four-and-a-half hours in four days

WITH THE WALL of death bike built and the record broken, I could spend more time training for the Tour Divide. I didn't know what I was letting myself in for. I knew it was 2,745 miles, alone and unsupported, only relying on what I could carry on my bike or my back.

I knew it involved the equivalent of cycling up seven Mount Everests. I knew that the people who set quick times were sleeping rough for four hours or less a day, but the only way you know if you can finish something like the Tour Divide is to try to do it. I wanted to get a feel for what it might be like, so I planned a training ride with Jason Miles, the top endurance mountain-bike racer that I broke the 24-hour tandem distance record with in 2014. We called it 'the coast to coast to coast'.

The idea was to ride from one coast of England to the far side of Scotland, get the ferry to Northern Ireland, then ride from the bottom to the top. We would treat it like I'd treat the Tour Divide: ride a bloody long way, sleep for a bit, ride some more. Not only did we want to leave the east coast and ride west, we also wanted to ride as many trail centres as we could do, and do the same in Ireland. Trail centres are purpose-built mountain-bike tracks that are dotted around the countryside. Some have nothing but a car park at the start and one or more signposted and maintained tracks through the woods to follow, others have cafés and bike shops and even elevated trail sections made from wood.

I chose Berwick-upon-Tweed, right on the Scottish border, as our start point. We would meet there late on the night of Wednesday 13 April. With the Tour Divide filling my head I came up with another idea. Any spare time I had I wanted to spend riding, so any way I could lengthen the ride I thought was a good idea. I worked late on Tuesday night, getting everything finished at the truck yard, and instead of driving up to Berwick, I reckoned I'd ride there to meet Jason.

So, at eight on Wednesday morning, I left home on the Salsa Fargo I planned to ride in the Tour Divide. This wasn't the first long ride I'd done in 2016. In January I set off from home, rode to the north of Scotland and, once I got there, had a night in a hotel before taking part in the Strathpuffer 24-hour mountain-bike race, which I'd done a few times before. It was cold and hard, dark and wet for most of the time, but what did I expect? It was January, in Scotland.

I rode on my Rourke single speed, so only one gear, meaning I had to slog up the hills in a gear higher than you might normally use. I'd ridden up through England on my own, but then 50 miles south of Edinburgh I met Alan, who, along with the Dungait brothers, I'd done a lot of biking with for years. We rode together from there up to Strathpuffer, a village in the Highlands, north of Inverness, where the event is held. On the way up the chain had totally dried out and was graunching like hell because of all the shit and blather. Alan had an idea to get some butter from a café to lubricate it.

The ride to the Strathpuffer was another thing I'd set my mind to do and it hadn't broken me, even though it was only a few months after the operation to bolt my

spine together. The weather wouldn't be as bad on the coast to coast to coast, but the mileage would be higher.

Leaving Grimsby, I didn't use a map. I was just riding off the compass on the Garmin, heading north. As long as I kept going that way I'd work it out. I rode over the Humber Bridge into Yorkshire, staying on small roads from then on. From Malton I knew a few back roads, and I knew that when I got to Northallerton I wanted to be heading more north-east, and then a bit north-west.

Last time I rode up this way, to the Strathpuffer, I went a bit further west, so this time I stuck east and headed towards the North York Moors. I got to the topside of Malton and followed true north on goat tracks. Five miles in, I was wondering if I'd done the right thing. It was a proper dirt track, which was alright, because I was on a mountain bike – a bit of an oddball-looking mountain bike, but built to cope with it. The bike was loaded up with sleeping bag, roll mats, inner tubes, chain, spare set of clothes and toothbrush. I didn't know where the trail would end, but I knew it wouldn't be a dead end. You never reach a dead end on a mountain bike because one dirt track always leads to another. The weather was spot on till one or two in the afternoon, then it pissed it down for most of the day and night. After 50 miles of these tracks, seeing no one, I came to a road with no idea where I was. I cycled into the nearest village and found out it was Great Ayton, near Guisborough. I was in Yorkshire, but only just, and right on the Cleveland border, eight miles from the centre of Middlesbrough.

It was four or five o'clock, and I found somewhere in the village to get loaded up with pork pies. I was loving the ride, even though I was soaked through. I had no one telling me what to do, no phone, and all I had to do was follow my compass and pedal north. It was great. It doesn't have to stop raining for long for you to dry out. I was wearing Lycra leggings with baggy shorts over the top; a Hope cagoule-type thing and Endura wool top; short socks; Endura gloves; and Sidi cycling shoes with old waterproof overshoes that I taped to my feet and only took off once in four days.

As I rode around Middlesbrough, the weather was misling – that drizzly, misty, soaking rain. I had the choice of bridle paths from Middlesbrough nearly to Newcastle, but they'd take me a fair way west before I got going north again. I'd been on them before and the Garmin will take me on them, but the A19 is true north. It's legal to ride a bike on this dual carriageway, but you're an idiot if you do. It's so dangerous – you're asking to get run over. But, I thought to myself, it's rush hour, the roads are heaving, so nothing is going too fast. Confirming that I am an idiot I set off towards Newcastle on the A19, and pedalled the 35 miles right to the Tyne Tunnel.

You're not allowed to ride a pushbike through the

Tyne Tunnel. You have to go into the office and they put the bike in a van and take you through. I'd met the maintenance lads in the office when I'd cycled up to the Strathpuffer in January, and they remembered me from then. I had a brew in their tea room.

I'd gone from Yorkshire with the 'Tha knows' accent, not seen anyone, then come out in Great Ayton, with a Middlesbrough accent, and now I was at the Tyne Tunnel with 'Hadoway and shite, champion man' Geordies. I'd only been on my bike half a day and I'd heard all these different accents.

It was seven or eight by the time I got through the Tyne Tunnel, and I knew Berwick was 70 or 80 miles north on B roads, so I decided to ride up the more direct way on the A1 rather than going on the coast road. Again, I was asking for trouble, pushbiking on such a fast and busy road, but I got away with it. And north of Newcastle the A1 isn't like it is south of the city. It's a two-way road for a lot of the way.

I reached Berwick after two on Thursday morning, 18 hours after leaving home.

I'm not a big McDonald's fan, but I'll stop in for tea if there's nowhere else, and I would spend a lot of time in McDonald's on this ride. Those 24-hour places are good when you're pushbiking like this. They're open, for a start, they've got bogs with hand driers, they're handy for loading up calories, and as long as you keep eating it doesn't matter what you look or smell like, they let you in. I chose the fattest thing I could see. I get the biggest burger with the most shit on it possible. What I realised on these rides was that every McDonald's plays the same music. It made me wonder, in a small way, what our world is coming to. It doesn't matter if you're in Northern Ireland or London, the music is the same. I imagined them having meetings at head office about what kind of music is going to be on next month's playlist. The answer is always the same: 'Just modern shit.' I kipped in the McDonald's for half an hour, with my forehead on the table, waiting for Jason.

When he arrived, having left home at one in the morning to drive up from Manchester, he unloaded his bike, parked his car where he was happy to leave it for three or four days, and we went over the plan quickly before setting off at five. The first part of the route was six hours on the road from Berwick to the first trail centre at Innerleithen. We met another lad, Sam, one of Jason's mates, who would do the rest of the Scottish part of the route with us.

Innerleithen, near Peebles, on the Scottish border, is one of the 7stanes mountain-bike trail centres on Scottish Forestry Commission land. There are eight locations, but Innerleithen and nearby Glentress are counted as one, and the trail centres are spread across the width of Scotland, all south of Glasgow and Edinburgh. The stane part of the name comes from the old Scottish word for stone, and there is a carved stone at each of the centres. There are trail centres all over Britain, but the 7stanes are some of the most popular – a big draw for folk from the whole of Scotland and beyond.

We weren't going hard at it, pacing ourselves for the rest of the ride, but we were going too hard to talk. The 11-mile loop around Innerleithen took summat like two hours. There wasn't a café or anything there, so we set off straight away to Glentress, only half an hour's ride down the road, for a good feed there. This is one of those trail centres with good facilities, like a bike shop, café, a bike-hire place and even showers. We only needed the café, and I had a jacket potato with everything you can get on it and a massive slice of cake. Anything with calories will do. I had been nibbling on pork scratchings all the time too. On a ride like this I get sick of eating. You're burning so many calories, and if you begin to feel hungry, it's too late. You can't let your body run into the reserve, because your energy has gone. Every bakery or butcher's I passed I would stop. I had an hour's kip at Glentress at the side of the road. I was out like a light. I hadn't slept since Tuesday night, and it was Thursday dinnertime. I wasn't hanging out my arse, but we knew we weren't going to make Newcastleton, the next trail centre, in the daylight, so it didn't matter if I had an hour's sleep.

I hadn't washed since Tuesday, and I was suffering with rashes from the stale sweat and dry skin – even up my nose was giving me grief. We left Glentress at four, heading for Newcastleton, 60 miles away to the south-east, in the middle of nowhere and in the opposite direction to the west coast we were aiming for.

We reached Newcastleton on B roads, arriving there at gone midnight. I put any extra clothes I had over what I was already wearing and swapped my cycling helmet for a woolly hat, before climbing into my sleeping bag at the side of the road. I didn't have a tent – I wouldn't take one on the Tour Divide, so there was no point. I had two or three hours' kip, but I was still cold. It felt like good practice for America.

We got up at first light, about five o'clock, and rode the Newcastleton trail for a couple of hours. People drive for hours to get to the trail centres for a pedal round, and I was enjoying riding them, even though the bike I was on wasn't the best tool for the job. It's got a hardtail, only 100 mm of front suspension travel and those handlebars, but it was going to have to do the same kind of riding that the trail centres would throw at it in America, so I wanted to give it stick to see what, if anything, broke on it or needed changing. Something like an Orange Gyro or Five, a full-suspension bike, would be better for the trail centres, a bike that deals with the ruts and bumps at speed. But they're heavier bikes, and that weight, multiplied over 2,745 miles and all that climbing, is no good. The Salsa I was riding had drop bars, called woodcutter bars, not regular mountain-bike bars, and it wasn't easy riding trails with them, but I had to try it. The benefit of the bars, with extra time-trialling bars bolted to them, is that they give a load of variation to where you can put your hands so you can change your body position and give yourself a rest. It's comfy, but the bike's slow because it's still a heavy bike compared to the one I'd use to race in the Strathpuffer.

We headed to the village shop to get breakfast. My method for deciding what to eat was picking up what looked tasty and comparing the weight of everything in my hand to see which was the heaviest. I picked up some custard slices, and they were heavy buggers, so I had them, thinking they'd be full of calories.

The next trail centre was Ae Forest, just west of the M74 near Dumfries. I had probably covered 350 or 400 miles since leaving home, and we had 40-odd miles and three hours to Ae. We stopped at a café for a banana milkshake, feeling under no pressure. I rang up Nutt Travel in Northern Ireland, to book a ferry.

At Ae we met Michael Bonney from Orange, the mountain-bike company. He was one of the top men there and I met him after I mentioned I had an Orange in a column for *Performance Bikes* years ago. Back in March 2013, Michael was out on a road ride with friends when he crashed his bicycle, just from a second's loss of concentration, and went off the side of the road. It wasn't anything unusual, the kind of crash people have all the time and climb back on their bike with nothing worse than a skinned knee, but Michael broke his neck and severed his spinal cord and was permanently paralysed from the neck down. A charitable trust was set up for him, and someone suggested our coast-to-coast-to-coast ride could become a way of raising money. I had no problem with that. I was doing the ride anyway, and we did it in aid of the Ride for Michael Trust.

There was a local TV crew at Ae Forest. I'm not sure how they happened to be there, but it must have been someone at the Trust who organised it. I'm not a big charity sort of man, but I have done plenty of stuff when it's meant something to me, and if it could help Michael out, then all well and good. He's had it hard and he's getting on with it, and I admire that. People had kindly donated money, and Michael got summat like £5,000 from the coast to coast to coast, I was told.

We didn't have time to ride the Ae Forest trail because we had to get to Cairnryan for the ferry. We missed the Kirroughtree trail centre too, because we were running a bit late and it was pissing it down. It was 85 miles to Cairnryan, and we had eight hours to do it. Now we were taking turns at the front, like they do in races like the Tour de France. The rider at the front is taking the brunt of the wind and those behind are riding close enough to be in the slipstream and have a slightly easier time of it. You do your bit at the front – don't go mad, only a few minutes – then pull out to the right so the other riders can come up the inside of you, and then you tag on the end, the place that's got the most aerodynamic benefit. You recover as best you can for another shift at the front. My arse was a bit sore by this point. I was trying a new seat. I'd always used SDG seats, but the Salsa came with a WTB and I quite liked it.

People go out for an 85-mile ride on a weekend and it would be a proper ride, but we had 85 miles to go in the dark to the ferry, and I'd already done 205 miles the first day and over 400 miles since leaving home. It was minus two with the wind chill and pissing it down. I wasn't cold while I was on the bike, but as soon as you stop it gets you.

Sam wasn't going to Ireland with us, so his dad met us at the ferry. We climbed in the back of his van and had a brew. Jason was shivering so much he was spilling his tea. He's as hard as nails, but he thought he was borderline hypothermic. He said, 'We have to get going.' He wasn't saying he wanted to stay in the van longer to get warm. He knew that getting back on the bike and starting pedalling again would be better.

We rolled on to the P&O ferry from Cairnryan to Larne. Cairnryan is near Stranraer, and if you've ever had to ride or drive there for the ferry to Ireland or the Isle of Man, you know it's a long way west.

We got another right feed on the ferry and the crew really looked after us. We were let into the lounge, and because we were soaking, one of the crew asked if we'd like our shoes putting in the drying room. There was complimentary wine, so me and Jason drank a bottle between us. Red wine has a good calorie value, so it was doing us good.

It was only a two-hour crossing, so there was next to no time to sleep, but I dropped off. The next thing: 'Bing-bong. Can drivers please return to their vehicles.' Fuck! We rolled off the ferry at two in the morning and a group of Irish lads I'd been talking to were there to meet us. Fair play to them, they were keen.

The Irish group were Geoff, Dave and Mike. They'd been training like hell since before August, and I got the feeling this was going to be like their Olympics. I only really knew Geoff before this. He worked for Chain Reaction Cycles, the massive mail-order company in Northern Ireland. He was the youngest of this group, in his mid-thirties, and he was one of the people behind the Ride for Michael Trust. Dave was late-forties and fit. He did 14,000 miles of cycling in 2015, so he's not a messer. Mike was between the other two in age, worked for Orange mountain bikes and came over from England for the ride. They were all riding mountain bikes, because that was the rule I'd made. Originally, my mate Tim was going to follow us in a van and we'd have road bikes for the road sections, then swap for mountain bikes for the trail centres, but I decided, a couple of weeks before, that it wasn't what I needed to do to prepare for the Tour Divide. I needed to test myself by having no support – just one bike and whatever I could carry.

Before we really got going, we biked to Geoff's house for Weetabix and tea, then we were back on the bikes at 5 am, heading south to a trail centre in the middle of Belfast, the Barnett trails.

We were aiming for some of the main trail centres in Northern Ireland. The next was Castlewellan, 40 miles south of Belfast, where we ate again and rode the trail. Next we headed over to Rostrevor, on the banks of Carlingford Lough, in Newry, right on the border. That was near-on 30 miles away, so after riding the trail it was time for another feed in the caff, then Jase and I had half an hour's kip on the grass bank outside. The sun was in the right place and I might have even got a bit sunburnt. I was absolutely knackered, but it was great. It felt like no one gave a damn about what we were doing. We were just five blokes out riding and I was loving it.

I didn't even know what day it was. I thought it was Friday, but it was Saturday. By the time we left Rostrevor it was five or six in the evening. We had more food outside Newry, probably four hours after the last feed. The chef came out, told us about the soup of the day and it sounded good, so I had that, thinking that I should give me guts something a bit easier to digest.

From the diner we headed to Davagh Forest trails, to the north-west of Cookstown, where the first motorcycle road race of the year is traditionally held, and a place that sometimes reminds me, after a long winter, of why I love road racing. This year was different. I wasn't racing until at least after the Tour Divide in June. The ride from Rostrevor to Davagh took us past Armagh, Portadown, Dungannon and Cookstown. It was all of 70 miles, and into a headwind, something we didn't need by this point.

We met a couple of lads I've known for years, Richard and Darren, who were supposed to ride with us, but we were later than we intended and it knackered up their plans. Instead, they sat in their van waiting for us for hours, then made us a much-needed cup of tea, but didn't bother riding. We got to Davagh Forest at some stupid time in the middle of the night. The ground was frozen, so we decided not to ride the trail. The Irish lads were suffering, but we kept at it, on to Desertmartin, Swatragh, Garvagh, Coleraine, Portrush. The last two towns being main points on the North West 200 course.

Just north of Swatragh I crashed, falling asleep while I was riding. My legs felt good and were still putting power out, but my brain needed a rest. I'd only slept

That's a Vulcan's landing gear. It's the one I taxied up and down a runway at Wellesbourne Airfield. I took this photo because it had a trick mechanical ABS system.

These are the Latvians who re-enacted Second World War battles. Some were German and some were Russians. The Latvians hated both sides, but they hated the Russians more.

That's the Lada that Kaspars gave a once-over with his expert eyes. It's parked outside my granddad's granddad's house. Great-great-granddad's? That's right, isn't it?

Some of the extended Kidals family I met in Latvia. Lovely people. They said I looked like a Kidals. You can see it, can't you?

At the Strathpuffer
on an Orange Gyro.

In the back of the van eating some of my mate Tim's special-recipe broth that he's perfected over years.

Handfuls of snacks to keep me going, supplied by Sharon.

More tea, vicar?

I'm taking off the fuel filter housing there.

In the pit at work.

The Indian Scout wall of death bike that Curly at Krazy Horse built.

My Rob North triple. This must have been the first day I turned up with it, because it doesn't have the cover over the clutch that they made me fit.

In Ken Fox's wall of death. Ken is on one of the Honda 200s I learned to ride the wall on.

This photo shows the scale of the wall we used to break the record. Directly below the folk on the viewing platform is the door in and out.

Being interviewed at the wall of death while Nigel looks on.

Looking down on the Rob North while stood next to Steve Jones, who presented the live programme.

My mum says
I'm special.

Me quizzing David
Coulthard and his
team to death while
a cameraman rigs
up the car.

That's Andy Spellman taking a
photo of me snoring like
a fog horn, or so he says.
I didn't hear anything.

four-and-a-half hours, or not much more, since I'd left home four days ago. I didn't hurt myself. I had kept slapping myself around the face, trying to keep myself awake, but it didn't work.

I explained to Jason that I wasn't weak-kneed, but I needed five minutes, so I slept in a bus shelter. I bet I was only sat on the floor for five seconds before I was asleep. I'd said I needed five minutes, and five minutes later Jason woke me up and said, 'Alright, let's get going.' I could've slept for eight hours, I bet, but that five minutes was enough to keep me going for another few hours. It was four or five in the morning, and not long after that forty winks the sun started coming up, which tricks the brain into thinking it's had more sleep that it has. Along the way we found a McDonald's. It was playing the same music, and that really annoyed me, but not enough to stop me from going in and filling my face.

We biked to Geoff's mum and dad's place in Portrush, right on the north coast of Northern Ireland. We were finished and still smiling. His parents weren't there, but his wife, Margaret, was and she cooked us steak and chips. From there, David took me and Jason to the ferry terminal in Larne in his car. I'd done over 750 miles by that point, so I wasn't wimping out by not riding to Larne. We had two hours on the ferry and it was chocka. A family in the corner had a right comfy bit and said we could sit with them, so we did and fell asleep. Sharon was waiting for us in the van at the ferry port when we docked at four in the afternoon. I climbed straight in the back of the van with the bikes and slept for four hours while she drove the 180 miles across the country to Berwick-upon-Tweed, where we dropped Jason off at his car. It was straight down the A1 for me and Sharon, and we got home at midnight. I went to work the next morning, in for eight. I didn't bike in. I was going to but Jason told me to have a few days' recovery, then have a big week the following week. I'd do a 50-hour week before the Tour Divide, then that would be it for serious training.

The longest I'd sat on a bike before this was the ride up to Inverness, which was a fair way, just over 500 miles, with over 100 miles of riding on the Strathpuffer itself. The coast to coast to coast was over 750 miles, from Wednesday morning to Sunday morning, and I'd learned a lot. The Rohloff hub I'd chosen wasn't the most precise thing, but it was reliable. My wheels needed to be lighter, because it took too long to accelerate. The bike was comfortable enough, but I needed to put more cream on my arse for saddle-sore. I needed more painkillers – nothing fancy, just ibuprofen, or vitamin I as some cyclists call it. When we were on the road, my arse and knees were getting sore and Jason was aching too, his back and arse, so he got on the painkillers and I asked, 'What are you doing with them?' He told me it just takes the edge off. I knew I had to take regular multivitamins to America, because you're eating so much fatty, greasy rubbish that you need vitamins to keep you right.

I learned that I know my pace. I know that when hills get steep I should get off and push for a bit, not kill myself every five minutes to make a climb, because if I do that I won't last. So I was pushing up hills in Ireland that I could ride up on a normal day's ride. You need a different mindset when you know you're cycling for 750 miles, or 2,745 miles. You've got to know that if you're only doing 3 or 4 mph and your heart rate is up to 180 or 190 bpm while you're crawling up the hill, you're not gaining anything. You can walk at that speed and get your heart rate down. And you have the added benefit that it stretches your legs. I only walked for five minutes or something at a time, until the gradient slackened off, then got back on. Jason would slog on, but that's him and he was on his featherweight race bike, not that I'm making excuses.

I also found that I couldn't eat enough. I did 55 hours of biking, at least 750 miles and 10,500 metres of climbing, and burnt something like 50,000 calories in just over four days. On the Tour Divide you've got to deal with self-cannibalisation, when the body has used up all the glycogen, the body's natural stored energy source, because you can't get enough food, and starts to eat at the muscles for energy. Tour de France riders can lose a lot of weight, but they're not riding long enough per day for self-cannibalisation to be a problem. The Tour de France is seen as the hardest race in the world, but the Tour Divide is more miles in less time, with no support and the riders sleeping rough, so you tell me what's the toughest race. Yes, the pace is slower, but Tour Divide riders are on the bike for more hours every day and it's a mountain bike, off-road.

This coast to coast to coast filled me with confidence, and I reckoned I could've done that pace for two weeks, which is what I'd have to do on the Tour Divide. It was scary thinking about it, but I was fascinated about what would be going through my mind at the end of it. Before then, though, I had a job on with a rebuilt Transit Custom.

CHAPTER 8

Legendary in the Transit world

THE TV BODS at North One were looking for ideas for stuff I could do for another series of *Speed*. A mate had told me about a couple of races in Nevada, flat-out, 90-mile time trials, held on closed public roads. The races are called the Silver State Classic Challenge and the Nevada Open Road Challenge. North One liked the sound of them.

When the TV lot started talking about a race in America, the idea turned to me doing the Nevada Open Road Challenge in a Transit van. Then everyone agreed it would be a lot better if it was done in a van that had some link to me, instead of one we might be able to get from Ford. They asked, 'Have you got a Transit van?' Well, actually, I have …

Between me, Andy Spellman and North One, we came up with the plan to turn the black Custom I'd written off and bought back from the insurance company into Supervan 4, and I'd go and race it out in Nevada. After everything that had gone wrong with the van, it sounded like it couldn't have worked out better.

Ford had been building promotional vans out of Transits since 1971, calling them Supervans. The first was a Mark 1 Transit fitted with a V8 engine from the famous Ford GT40 sports car.

Built in 1984, Supervan 2 had a version of a Cosworth DFV V8 F1 engine, rear-mounted on a Ford C100 Group C racing-car chassis with the fibreglass body of a Mark 2 Transit over the top. Really, it was a Le Mans racing-car chassis with an F1 engine in it and a fibreglass shell. It would do 174 mph, but it wasn't really usable. The engine was so highly strung that it needed pre-heating before you could start it, and a team of mechanics to look after it whenever it ran anywhere. And Ford had used a body shape that was just about to be replaced with a new production van, so, from a marketing point of view, it was out of date not long after being built. It was only used for a year before it was retired.

Supervan 3 appeared in 1994 and was used to promote the new Mark 5. It had a seven-eighths scale fibreglass body and was originally fitted with a Cosworth HB V8 F1 engine, the same type that powered Michael Schumacher's Benetton when he won his first F1 title in 1994. The Supervan's engine was eventually replaced with a Ford Cosworth 3-litre V6, so it could be more usable. Mine could be thought of as Supervan 4, making it legendary in the Transit world.

North One decided they'd use Krazy Horse to manage the building of the van. The company's boss, Paul Beamish, is really into his hot rods and American muscle cars. The shop is also a Morgan dealer, so they had the facilities and mechanics to do it. The TV lot trusted Krazy Horse because they'd proved how hard they worked on the wall of death, and they were on the same wavelength.

The van would be completely modified: V6 twin-turbo engine; converted from front- to rear-wheel drive; roll cage; massive brakes; coil-over suspension.

There are different classes to enter in the Nevada Challenge race. You tell the organisers which class you want to run in – 100 mph, 140, 150 or unlimited – and I was going to be in the 150 mph class. The idea is to cover the 90-mile course at as close to an average of 150 mph as possible, but it's harder than it sounds. I was told that in the 2015 race, a boy who was summat like two-tenths of a second off the perfect time for averaging 150 mph over the 90-mile course wasn't even in the top 20.

I had no idea how I was going to drive 90 miles that accurately. I would have a local co-driver, or navigator, as they call them in this race, a man who knows where to go steady and where to give it the berries. And the race was in May, so not even two months after the wall of death attempt I would be going to America to race what might be the world's fastest van. I just hoped there wouldn't be any parked car transporters in the way.

At the beginning of December 2015, my wrecked Transit Custom, FT13 AFK, was collected and taken to Krazy Horse in Bury St Edmunds, Suffolk. I followed it for the first day of filming on the *Speed* programme. Paul Beamish, his salesman Stuart, who has built hot rods all his life, and Krazy Horse's mechanic Dan Sims were there, and some wild ideas were chucked about. Ford V8s and rear-mounted turbos were all discussed before a plan was decided while the cameras filmed it all.

The next day the van was taken to Baker Body Craft in Mildenhall, a specialist body-repair company that Krazy Horse trust. They set about straightening the van and ended up putting an A-pillar in it. An A-pillar is the upright that runs from the sill, has the door hinges fasten to it then forms the side windscreen frame and carries on to join the roof panel. You know a car or van is near enough buggered if it needs an A-pillar in it.

I went back to the wall of death job that was looming, while Dan got on with the Transit. He would be the foreman in charge of modifying my van. I would have loved to do it, but it was being built at the same time that I was flat out with the wall of death bike, so I didn't lay a hand on it. Dan was the brains behind the whole job. He's 32 and a real good lad. He had worked as a Mercedes mechanic for 13 years, starting out as an apprentice and working up to diagnostic technician on all vehicles, from smart cars up to Sprinter vans and everything in between, including AMG Mercs. He'd been at Krazy Horse just short of a year when he started on the Transit.

He set about putting meat on the bones of the plan while Craig McAlpine, one of the subby researchers at North One, contacted Ford GB to tell them what we were doing. Craig's in his mid-twenties and dead into his cars, so he was the ideal man for this job. Ford offered North One a special Tourneo, the minibus version of the Transit, that their motorsport department had fitted with a 400-horsepower V6 EcoBoost engine, a six-speed manual gearbox and a Ford F-150 pick-up back axle. Tourneos are only ever front-wheel drive, like Transit

Customs, but Ford's motorsport lads had wanged this eff-off engine, Mustang gearbox and a back axle in it for the fun of it. It had been chucked together by some of the mechanics – a few of them had been involved in the Supervan projects – but it was never supposed to see the light of day. It was only ever a tea-break and after-work project – an experiment – that was never meant to be anything fancy. We were told that the Tourneo project had been shelved, but they were happy to help us.

Ford were never going to do anything with this special van, except crush it, so they told the TV lot that we could take whatever we needed off it. Dan took the ideas from the Tourneo, but not a lot more, then did it his own way.

On 28 January, Dan took the Tourneo to Millbrook Proving Ground, the specialist automotive industry test facility, near Bedford, to see what it could do. He got 138.5 mph on the bowl before he reckoned it felt a bit loose at the rear. It clocked 125 mph at the end of a mile from a standing start and 135 mph on a flying mile. The test gave us half an idea about the gear ratios we'd need to run top speeds and proved that a Transit would do 140 mph with a bog-standard EcoBoost engine. Ours would end up being a lot neater job, though.

Our van, FT13 AFK, was coming along slowly but steadily, though there was a problem. North One reckoned that the van couldn't be imported into America without a logbook, and because it was a Category B, it no longer had a valid logbook. Baker's had finished the repairs on the van and done a perfect job of it. The TV researchers found out that they could have the van rebuilt, then inspected, and pay for an engineer's report to prove the van was as good as new. Spellman had to smooth it out with the insurance company, who'd already sent me a cheque for the written-off Transit. It would have been a lot easier to start with a different van, but then it wouldn't have been mine and I wouldn't have been as into it. The engineer's report did the job and Spellman got the van reclassified from Category B to C, meaning we could use the van for the project. Another hoop had been jumped through.

Dan and Craig from North One had been contacting parts suppliers to see what they could get in time for the project. The timescale for something as complicated and oddball as a 175-mph Transit van was dead tight, and some of the specialist companies they got in touch with were too stacked out to help. Eventually, with only about three months before it would have to be shipped out to America, Krazy Horse could really start on the spannering.

At first we were going to use the engine out of the Tourneo, but it was a really early prototype engine and nothing else we planned to use wanted to fit it, so Dan decided we should start from scratch with a different motor. Because he was talking to loads of different parts suppliers for the van, through this man and that man, a deal was done with Radical to supply an engine and other parts.

Radical are a sports car company based in Peterborough. They started in 1997, making track cars powered by superbike engines. The cars were for keen track day drivers, very lightweight, dead revvy and adjustable, so they were more like proper racing cars than modified road cars. And because they had motorcycle engines and fibreglass or carbon-fibre bodywork, they had good power-to-weight ratios. From very early in their history, Radical organised their own race series for owners, and they quickly started exporting around the world.

The company kept adding models, eventually making a road-legal car, all the time with bike engines, then, in 2005, they started using the Ford V8 engine in their SR8. That car – it looks like a modern Le Mans racer – holds the production-car lap record at the Nürburgring Nordschleife, the place I'd still like to go back to with a trick motorbike for a crack at the lap record. It's on the list. By the time they got involved with our Transit project, Radical had built over 2,000 cars in their 19-year history.

The engine they promised us was a twin-turbo V6 EcoBoost, and supposedly good for 700 horsepower. If you're not familiar with horsepower figures, a 2015 Ferrari 458 only makes 562 horsepower, while a 2015 Porsche 911 Turbo is 572 horsepower.

By the middle of February, FT13 AFK was returned to Krazy Horse with the front half of a steel roll cage that had been fitted by Safety Devices. Think of a roll cage as a strengthening skeleton that fits inside a vehicle. Formula One and Le Mans 'prototype' racing cars are designed to survive very fast crashes, but road cars and vans are only tested up to a certain speed. If they're then converted for racing they usually need extra crash protection. Our roll cage is made from steel tube, about the same diameter as a scaffold pole, welded together and then welded to the van's chassis.

Safety Devices made a rear roll cage that would also be used to mount the much-improved suspension to. The standard Transit has a leaf-spring back axle, but because we were increasing the power so much we needed a different set-up, and we used a four-bar linkage. The leaf spring is fine for regular van work, but Dan felt our Supervan needed something more sophisticated that would be able to deal with high-speed cornering. The van would be lowered about two inches and set up a lot more level than a regular Transit. As standard, the rear of the Transit sits higher than the front, so that when it's carrying a load it's not driving around with its front end in the air.

With the four-bar set-up you have a swingarm with tie-bars connecting it to the chassis of the van. The tie-rods are connected to coilover units – where the spring coil is over the shock – that supply the suspension and damping. Even though this is a conventional set-up for some modern cars, we had nothing to mount the top of the shock to because the Transit was never designed to have it. Dan cut the front suspension turrets out of the Tourneo and made them into top shock mounts for the rear of our Transit, and these were incorporated into the roll cage. Safety Devices also strengthened the chassis behind the dash so the van almost had a space-frame chassis, making it stiff and safe. It's trick.

While the chassis was being modified, Radical were fettling the new engine. They fitted Carrillo con rods, JE pistons and their own inlet manifolds. Twin Garrett GTX2871R turbos had been sent to Radical to fit to the 3.5-litre EcoBoost V6. Radical had tried to get a Quaife gearbox sorted but there wasn't time to make it, so we had to settle for the donor 'box from the Tourneo, which was out of one of Ford's American pick-ups.

Back at Krazy Horse, a rear wing from a Le Mans car had been supplied by Wirth Research. I met two of their design engineers, Adam Carter and Stuart Ciballi, who had both worked for F1 teams before joining Wirth. They had done some computational fluid dynamics simulations, where a computer program predicts the flow of air over an object – in this case my van. They advised us to mount the wing in a specific position and angle. They also supplied mounts to withstand 700 kg of downforce. The point of the wing was to stick the van to the road at high speed, but there was the potential for so much downforce that we'd need to bolt it to extra strengthening mounts welded on the inside of the back doors, or they'd buckle when the van really got shifting and the aerodynamic force started pushing the van on to the road surface.

I had a go in Wirth's race simulator to get a feel for driving fast. I've owned a few fast cars, done a Caterham race and a few track days, and the Volvo, my turbo six-cylinder Amazon, has taught me a few things about driving quickly, but I don't think I'm Lewis Hamilton.

Dan built a frame for the front air dam and sent it to motorsport bodywork specialists KS Composites in Leicestershire, who covered it with Twintex, a flexible material that's summat like carbon fibre, but more flexible. The front air dam is basically the front bumper, but Wirth suggested the shape that would work best with the aerodynamics of the van. It had to have an opening for the radiator and turbo intercoolers, and that opening was made bigger later.

Before the brakes and suspension had arrived, the TV lot needed a mock-up of how the van would look so they could get approval from the EPA, the Environmental Protection Agency, to enter the US for the race. Dan covered the framework in cardboard and duct tape, put the wheels and old suspension on and painted the lights to make it look as much like a racing car as possible. North One took photos and sent them off. The van needed a visa to get into the USA, and I did too.

I had to visit the American Embassy in London with Andy Spellman, getting there at eight in the morning and waiting in line. There aren't any specific appointments – it's first come, first served. I was called to the window and asked what I did for a living. I told the fella, like I tell everyone, that I'm a truck fitter, but this wasn't what he wanted to hear, because I was applying for a work visa to make a TV programme. I was told to sit in a corner and wait. So I waited. And waited. Then I got a call from Spellman, who was waiting outside, asking what was happening. A short while later my name was called and I got told that everything had been approved and I'd be given the work visa I needed to go to America and film the programme. Spellman had pulled some strings. I've no idea what he did or who he spoke to, but I'm glad he did.

By now the van still looked a lot like mine from the outside, but it was totally different under the skin. As well as welding in the front suspension turrets from the Tourneo, Dan notched the chassis rails so it could be converted to rear-wheel drive. The standard petrol tank wasn't up to the job, so two 120-litre ATL racing-car fuel cells were fitted in the back. The brakes were converted to CompBrake 350 mm discs with 6-piston calipers and the wheels were M-Sport OZs. The organisers recommended a tyre-pressure monitoring system to give an early warning of a tyre going down, before it blew out, and Dan arranged for bf1systems to fit one. Also on the safety side of things, a Lifeline automatic fire-extinguisher system was fitted. It had Cobra racing seats and Schroth Racing harnesses and HANS systems. The Transit really was short of nowt.

The Tourneo was left-hand drive, but my van was regular UK right-hand drive, so Dan had to muck about swapping over the power-steering gubbins, then the van went off to Demand Engineering in Stowmarket for new turbo headers and side-exit exhausts. There were probably two-dozen companies involved in converting the van.

Because it was a bit of a rush job to get the van ready in time to go out to Nevada for the race in May, we only had one chance to test it in England, and I put a spanner in the works by cocking up the diary dates and forcing Krazy Horse and Radical to get the van ready a day early.

The test was planned for Bruntingthorpe in Leicestershire, a privately owned former airbase that was now used as a proving ground by manufacturers and magazines. It has a runway that's nearly two miles long, so it's about the best top-speed test track in Britain. But I'd double-booked myself for the Friday test day. I'd entered the Scottish two-day Pre-65 motorcycle trial, being held in Fort William at the back end of April, thinking it was a Saturday and Sunday, but it was Friday and Saturday. I'd been asked to ride it by the folk at Hope, who were one of the event's sponsors, and didn't want to miss it, so the TV lot set about changing everything from Friday to Thursday. It was my fault this time. I couldn't blame anyone for writing it in the back of my diary when it should have been in the front. Bugger. My cock-up meant Radical would lose a day of fettling when they were already up against it. And the whole job was behind schedule anyway, so it was now too late to put the van in a container and ship it out to America. It would have to be flown to Las Vegas, a bloody expensive way of going about things.

After we finished filming, I got back in the hire van (my grey Transit was in for repairs) and drove to Bruntingthorpe. I got there just before midnight and kipped in the front of the van, happy to sleep there instead of mucking about getting a hotel.

My mate Dobby knew I was testing the Transit, so he took a day off work and drove down in his own Transit and we had an early-morning fry-up in the Bruntingthorpe café.

The van was supposed to be there at eight in the morning, but it wasn't. It turned out that Radical had been running the van on their dyno overnight before the test to start setting up the fuelling maps, but they reckoned that the heat in the dyno room had cooked the starter motor. The test was postponed until midday, but then the oil cooler split as they were loading the Transit on to the transporter to leave Peterborough. They finally got it sorted at two in the afternoon, but were still about two hours away, so we mucked about until they turned up. Dobby was in his Transit Custom, Nat the cameraman had his Mercedes Vito 116 that he thought was rocket-fast, and I was in a hired Vauxhall. We had the two-mile runway to ourselves and nothing else to do until the souped-up Transit arrived from Radical, so we started racing our vans. I'd never do it in my own van, but as it's a rental, let's go mental! Dobby's was the quickest. It would do 105 mph before the speed limiter cut in. Then Spellman came in his M-Sport Transit. His had similar acceleration to Dobby's up to 105, but, because his speed limiter had been taken off and the engine remapped to give more horsepower, it would keep going until 115 mph.

Eventually, we got a phone call saying, 'We're just leaving,' and I was thinking, I need to be in Fort William. Originally, I had to be in Scotland before seven on Thursday evening. I explained what was happening and they said they'd let me sign on the next morning, but I still had to get to Fort William, and that was seven-and-a-half hours away on a perfect run without stopping.

The Transit finally turned up at about half-five. From the outside it just looked like my van, but with black wheels and a big wing on the back, which is good because I didn't want it to look all Carlos Fandango. The starting procedure was totally different to the last time I'd driven it too. I had to turn the ignition on, to energise everything, then flick the master switch to turn the ECU on, then switch the fuel pumps on, before pressing a button to start the engine.

I started testing the van and soon worked out that the two-mile runway was long enough for it to rev out in fifth gear – when I put it into sixth the power just died. It didn't feel like a 700-horsepower motor to me, but that could've been the gearing making it feel that way. There was a massive gap between fifth and sixth gear – I'd lose 2,000 rpm changing up, so the motor would drop out of the boost and lose all its momentum, meaning I had to shift down again. I was left thinking, Well, that isn't fast enough. I knew how much work everyone had put into it all, but I was only getting 145 mph out of the twin-turbo, 3.5-litre V6, and I wasn't very impressed.

In the 150 mph class of the Nevada Open Road Challenge you aren't allowed to drop below 145 (after getting up to speed) or go faster than 165. So, obviously, the Transit had to do more than 150 to average that speed, when you take the standing start and corners into the equation.

Still, the fellas from Radical weren't panicking. They were just saying, 'Well, we'll give it more boost,' and I thought, But it won't pull top gear. Why don't you muck about with the back axle ratio? (This is a bit like changing the rear sprocket on a motorbike.)

After a couple of hours in the van it was time to call it a day. The Transit was loaded back on to the transporter and I headed off to Fort William. I ended up going Stoke way, up the M6, M74 and A9. The A82 around Loch Lomond was closed overnight, so I had to go right up the other side of Scotland. I bet I was only 60 miles short of Inverness before I turned towards the west and started heading back down towards Fort Bill. I got to the A9 and it was snowing like hell and settling, so I had a couple of hours' sleep in the van, near Stirling, and got to Fort William at five in the morning. I had another couple of hours' sleep in the van, then went to the B&B, had breakfast with the lads from Hope and rode the trial.

How did I do in the trial after all that? Shit.

CHAPTER 9

No one's putting the right pair of sunglasses on before being photographed

TWO WEEKS AFTER the Bruntingthorpe test, on Tuesday 10 May, I was on a flight to America to take part in the Nevada Open Road Challenge, which would take place on the Sunday, 15 May. The Transit had been flown out to Las Vegas and, because it still wasn't 100 per cent right, Dan from Krazy Horse and Craig from North One had gone out a couple of days earlier than me and the rest of the TV lot to carry on fettling it.

The Transit had been transported from the airport to Radical Ventures, an independent garage just outside of Vegas that sells the British-built Radical track cars. Their mechanics had changed the van's back axle ratio and fuel pump, and stiffened up the shocks with springs flown in from Intrax in the UK, which was all done before Dan and Craig arrived. But the van had also developed clutch trouble.

The clutch was a bit of an unknown, because when Radical use this engine in their track cars they use a different gearbox and a smaller flywheel. The Radicals are mid-engined, so the propshafts run off the gearbox. The Transit's V6 is in the front and has a Mustang gearbox bolted to it, and it needs a driveshaft to a rear differential that drives the back axle. Radical didn't have much experience with this set-up.

The gears were a bit vague when I was testing it at Bruntingthorpe – the linkage didn't feel right, but it wasn't any bother. The trouble with the clutch came when it was being unloaded from the transporter. Whoever was shunting it off the truck frazzled the clutch, so it obviously wasn't right, and they had done us a favour buggering it in time for us to do something about it.

When the lads checked it they found that the clutch was properly knackered. It was replaced with a clutch from a five-litre Mustang that happened to be in the garage. Once it was back together it was still making an unhealthy noise, so they stripped it again and saw that the clutch's main bearing was damaged. We were all there by now. James from Radical had flown out with us, and between him and Dan they reckoned the problem was down to using a prototype clutch that had come from the Tourneo, so they swapped it again.

James and Dan did all the spannering, but I'd have preferred to be in their position, getting my hands dirty. They had the gearbox in and out, in and out, in and out. They ended up putting a Shelby twin-plate racing clutch in, and that cured it. It caused more expense too. Shelby are the legendary Ford tuners who became famous for building and racing Mustangs and Cobras back in the 1960s. It was lucky they were also based in Las Vegas.

On the Wednesday, the day after we landed in America, the lads were still sorting the clutch, and the North One lot wanted to do some TV bullshit with me and Paul and Stuart from Krazy Horse. They had us riding around Vegas on Victory V-twins, big cruiser bikes. Stuff like this is sometimes filmed and not used – I'd done some filming on a 1980s BMW when I was riding around Latvia that never made it into the programme – but it's better to have it and not need it than be looking for it if something goes wrong further down the line. The ride was alright, but I was beginning to feel like a bit of a TV wanker, because I wasn't working on the van – the other lads were. It didn't sit right.

That night we did more filming, in the older part of Las Vegas, around Fremont Street. I'm not into Vegas, but I was getting to see stuff I don't normally see. I had a mooch about, the camera following me as I did what I thought was interesting to film, instead of being told, 'Go and talk to this man.' It was like the stuff I did in India, when I visited the truck yard and spoke to the old bloke cutting valve seats and the woman who changed the tyres. I like doing that now and I'm half-comfortable with the camera. I've always worked with the same TV crew from the very first boat programme, and we get on well. I don't feel awkward in front of them and they know what to say to me to get what they need. I spoke to Fremont Street buskers. There was a man and woman dressed as pirates, and she had the biggest tits I'd ever seen. There were three blokes using cooking-fat drums and bits of metal as drums, and they were brilliant. There was a good street magician too.

Because I was a newcomer to the race I had to attend a rookie school at six in the morning on Thursday at the Las Vegas Speedway. It was partly in the classroom, and then we had to drive on the track to show we could drive a car. The race is open to all folk, so they have to make sure, I suppose. The Transit was still being worked on so I borrowed a Ford Mustang from Frank, who is a racer and one of the organisers of these Nevada races, and also the uncle of John Putnam, who'd been lined up to be my navigator for the race.

After the course we went to check on the van, and the lads had it all back together and seemed happy with it. I took it for a short test drive, which the TV lot were very unhappy about because I wasn't insured, but the van felt right.

The TV bods look after me. They rented me a pushbike, so I could go cycling early in the morning. Just 30 or 40 miles to keep my eye in. I knew the Tour Divide would fail or succeed on these mornings, and I just wanted to keep my legs turning.

We moved to Ely, where the race was based, after a couple of nights in Las Vegas. The TV lot had a local fixer working for them, like they use on a lot of the foreign jobs. A fixer is someone who knows the local landscape and businesses and can get things done – a person who knows a man who knows a man. The fixer fixed it for us to take the Transit to a runway in Eureka, 70-odd miles west of Ely, for a last-minute test. The runway was a mile-and-a-half long, so plenty of room to test the clutch and anything else.

Eureka is 6,000 feet up, surrounded by snowcapped mountains, but a real one-horse town of about 600 people. The bloke who ran the airfield said that planes didn't normally bother telling him in advance if they were planning to land, so we had to keep an eye out. Normally, you have to pay the paramedics on a job like this. The TV lot dot the i's and cross the t's, doing pages and pages of risk assessments to make everything as safe as possible, and part of it all is having the right professional cover in place, like paramedics, firemen or whatever. It's all about covering backsides and making sure that if something does go wrong, every reasonable effort has been made to guarantee it's dealt with properly. North One aren't trying to stop me doing stuff – it's the opposite. For this test the local paramedics turned up and didn't even want paying. They were just happy to be on standby and see what was going on.

We had a regular Ford Transit to get around in when we were out there, but it was a size you can't get in England. The smallest one in America is L1 H1, only a little bit bigger than a Transit Custom (which isn't really a proper Transit; the smallest proper Transit in Britain is the L2 H2 – that's a longer wheelbase, higher top than the American one). The van we'd borrowed had a V6 in it. Ford don't sell the Transit Custom in America, the model our race van was built out of.

The race van was following us from Ely on a transporter driven by Nam, a Chinese fella, who didn't speak a lot of English, but was a good bloke. I razzed up and down, up and down in the Transit we were using as our regular transport until Nam turned up, then I got into the race van and cracked on.

Similar to what we'd seen at the Bruntingthorpe test, our Transit would only do 148 mph before I ran out of runway and had to start braking. It was pulling sixth now, though, and still accelerating, but we were going into the race not knowing what it was capable of. I thought it would do over 150, but I was beginning to get the inkling that we'd come a long way to not go as fast as we thought we would. I was feeling a bit pessimistic but I kept my gob shut. The lads working on the job were more confident. The good news was that the van behaved itself, but everything was running a bit hot.

When we were driving back from Eureka we had to stop while real cowboys and cowgirls herded cattle over the road on horses.

Amateur races in America, like the Nevada Open Road Challenge, get the local towns involved with their events. I'd seen it at Colorado Springs, the nearest big town to Pikes Peak, and it was the same here. On Friday there was a car parade through Ely, starting at the school, with all the racing cars driving through the town with the locals and tourists lining the street. Ely has a few casinos and stuff, and is a nice enough place, but it's a bit backwards. We were taught blackjack in an Ely casino for the TV cameras.

After the parade there was a car show, held outside the local knocking shop, the Stardust Ranch, for the Hookers' Choice competition. I don't have any experience with brothels, but this was like a bar – a tidy, well-used bar, but with women not wearing a lot schmoozing about. It wasn't like Grimsby's Chicago Rock Cafe that my sister Sal and I used to work in, but it didn't scream 'whorehouse' either. It was far from a shithole.

The lasses looked like they'd done some miles and they had a few quid on them, meaning they thought they looked the business. I suppose they have to in that game. Prostitution is legal in some counties of Nevada – not the whole state – and it was obviously legal here, so the business wasn't hidden, like it is at a 'massage parlour' in Grimsby.

The custom show was judged by the women who worked at the brothel. They looked around the cars and picked the one they'd most want to get shagged in. It was strange to have a race with a parade that had started off at a school and was now having custom cars being judged by prostitutes, but that's what happened. The Transit won, but I was asleep in the van when they were handing out the prizes, and Paul and Stu from Krazy Horse collected the trophy.

On Saturday, the day before the race, I met with John Putnam, my navigator. We took his uncle Frank's 2008 Mustang for a recce of the race route. John is in his early fifties, the president of a geology and topographic mapping company. He's a big bloke, nice, polite and clean-shaven. He lives in Oregon, not far from Matt Markstaller, the man behind the Triumph streamliner. His uncle Frank is one of the main men behind the Silver State Classic Challenge and Nevada Open Road Challenge races. Frank's Mustang had been sat in Vegas for a few weeks after being driven back from the Chihuahua Express, another race like the one I was entered in, that is held down in Mexico. Both John and Frank had competed in it. Frank owned a casting company that made stuff for Freightliner trucks, the same company Matt Markstaller worked for.

It took us four hours to do the recce, because the course is 90 miles long and you have to drive back to the start. John was zeroing his rally computer, which was calibrated to the wheel speed. The course is a bit boring, being mainly straight with just a few little bends in it. And if you get caught speeding in the month up to the event you are disqualified, so I was going dead steady.

Back in Ely the van was being scrutineered to check it was safe to race. Krazy Horse Paul reckoned some of the race organisers didn't really get what we were trying to do with the van. They couldn't understand why we didn't just do it in a car. If I had to explain, you wouldn't understand. Because of that they were nitpicking over the van, but it passed. I didn't have the same experience.

The folk I met said stuff like, 'You've come all the way from England to race a van? Fair play.'

There were also some grumblings that I'd been let straight into the 150 mph class even though I was a rookie. All newcomers are usually limited to something like the 110 mph class, so it was a bit controversial.

After the recce, the night before the race, Dan and James decided to rip back into the van again in the car park of the hotel. They wanted to move the radiators and intercoolers to help with the cooling of the engine. They removed the mesh from the front bumper and repositioned the carbon-fibre bumper to try to allow some more air into the engine. I was there watching them for a bit, trying to help, but there was only room for two and I was a spare pair of hands that weren't needed, so the rest of us went to get a steak. I ordered one the size of a car bonnet.

The race was an early start, probably to cause the least amount of disruption. I was up at five, we met on the street at six, then the 100-odd cars that had entered all drove in a convoy with a police escort for the 30-odd miles to Lund, where the race starts. Some of the cars aren't road legal, but most are modern sports cars, Mustangs, a few old muscle cars. The drivers are gentlemen racers, old boys with money driving Lamborghini Diablos, and Dodge Hellcats, the most powerful production muscle car ever, with 707 horsepower from the factory.

I had all my gear on: proper driving boots, fireproof overalls. I had to use a car helmet, not my regular AGV, because car helmets have fireproof linings (though a fireproof lining might have been a good idea for at least one of my bike helmets). John and I had intercoms in our helmets so we could hear each other at 150 mph.

Like I've explained, the race is a time trial and run in classes, the winner of each being the closest to the perfect time of their class's designated speed. So if it took 38 minutes and 10 seconds to cover the course at that speed, the winner is the closest to that time. We could change our class at the eleventh hour, if we wanted, and go in with the 145 mph lot, 130 or whatever. I still wasn't feeling optimistic, and maybe that was because I hadn't been working on the van. I didn't doubt Dan and James, but the van had never done the speeds it had to do. I spoke to Krazy Horse Paul, wondering what he thought I should do. He said, 'Go in the 150 class. What's the worst that can happen?' And that was it.

The 150 mph class, with me in it, went first, followed by the 90 mph lot. After them, the 180 mph group were flagged off. The 150 mph class had 16 entries, the second most after the 110 mph bracket, which had 18 cars entered in it.

As soon as we left the line I had my head on, like I was going road racing. I was listening out for John's notes, 'Fast, sweeping left, going into tight section right.'

There's a bit of driving to be done, but not much.

The upper speed limit for our class was 165 mph, with a lower limit of 145, to stop people doing the route at 190 then parking in front of the line and crawling over right at the perfect time for the 150 mph average.

As soon as we got over 100 mph the wing mirrors blew in. The van no longer had its regular Transit mirrors – it had fancy, and much smaller, Formula Two things. With the mirrors folded in, I couldn't see if anything was coming behind us.

I wasn't nervous, but I didn't know how the van was going to deal with the bends because it was top heavy. On the recce we'd gone through some of the bends at 75 or 80 mph in the Mustang, and I told John, 'If we can't do these at 150 mph in our Transit we've got problems,' because they were such slight bends. I soon found that it wasn't so straightforward when I went through some sweepers at 150 mph and knew about it. The way to deal with corners was not to drive through on a steady part-throttle, but to back off the throttle before the bend, then get back on it going through to keep the van accelerating and settled on its suspension. It seemed to like that more.

The Transit's new twin-turbo V6 revved to over 7,000 rpm, which is a lot when you think I hardly ever go over 2,000 rpm in a Transit normally.

We were burning two gallons of pump petrol for every mile when we were flat out. That's why we needed

200-odd litres. The Volvo is worse than that. When it's on song you couldn't tip it away faster. Nothing drinks it quicker than that Volvo.

I had enough time to think this was a mega thing to be doing. It was the first time we had it close to flat out, because everywhere we'd tested was an airfield, with a maximum length of two miles and a dead stop or a tight bend at the end. They weren't long enough to allow the Transit to slowly but steadily accelerate to reach its top speed. It was different out on the Nevada roads – I could just keep it nailed. Up until that point I thought the Transit could only do 150 mph, and I was just concentrating on the job, until I heard John the navigator in my helmet intercom saying, 'You'd better back off – you're doing 170.' The 'tech' speed for the 150 mph class was 165, so if I'd gone through one of the speed traps at 170 we'd have been disqualified. The van felt like it had more to give, so it might have a 175 mph top speed as it is now. It took three miles of constant acceleration to get above 150 mph.

In the Transit's class was a Ford Mustang, nine Corvettes, a Lamborghini, a Nissan 350Z, a Mercedes AMG, an Ultima GTR and a Dodge Viper. Every competitor in the 150 mph class was within 1 mph of the target average speed, and that was over a 90-mile-long route. The 150 mph class is the toughest. Anything faster needs a load of expensive kit installing, like a fire-extinguisher system in the cab and under the bonnet, a full roll cage and five-point harnesses. You're allowed in the 150 mph with regular seatbelts and a small roll cage. One bloke was racing a Ferrari F40, a million quid car, in the 110 mph class.

Once I was in top gear I didn't need my foot planted on the floor. When it was up to speed I could back off the throttle and just hold it there, at 160 mph. On the boost it didn't really matter where the throttle was. Driving like that made everything a bit smoother. It would rev to 7,000 rpm through the gears, but it wouldn't in top gear. With that differential ratio it was geared to do 200 mph, but it didn't have the power to rev out in top gear, so that speed was just theoretical. I can't think of another race where you'd go so fast for so long without backing off for a corner.

I had a timer by my side, showing us where we were in relation to the perfect 150 mph run. At one point we were 20 seconds behind schedule, but we were doing 165 mph so clawing back the time.

There's one section, 20 miles from the end, called the Narrows, where there are some twisties for about two miles and you can drop below the lower 'tech' speed. I didn't want to push it through there – I'd have looked like a right wanker if I'd crashed.

I crossed the line at perfect zero on my timer, but 100 metres before the finish line John's computer zeroed to a reference point he had and told us that we were actually eight seconds out. It was probably down to the expansion of the tyre. Our start time was 8.16am, and the perfect time for the run was 36 minutes. We were 36 minutes and 8 seconds. That's going some to cover 90 miles – in a van. My target speed was a perfect 150 mph, but the actual speed was 150.5789 mph. It doesn't sound too bad, does it? But the winning speed was 150.001 mph, set by Robert Wood, driving a British Ultima GTR, a British supercar, with a Chevy V8 engine that you can buy ready to drive or in kit form. They reckon it was the fastest accelerating production car in the world when they launched it. Wood didn't have a navigator, but he looked like he had half a NASA space station on the passenger side of his dashboard. He was working with Atomic time, like the timekeepers of the race did. If you're working from GPS it depends on what satellite you're getting the signal from if you have a delay or not. There's more to it than that, but fair play.

Our Transit had all the safety gear you needed to enter the unlimited class, but it would have got smoked. The fastest unlimited class car was a Chevrolet NASCAR with a fibreglass body over a spaceframe, powered by a normally aspirated, great big V8, running on slick tyres. It went through the speed trap at 233.8 mph and averaged 209.9 mph. The owner had to put a different back axle in it to work on the road, because they're built for going around banked oval tracks, and the camber of the wheels is strange because of that. Even at those speeds he didn't break the course record. That still stands at an average of 217.5570 mph set by Jim Peruto, driving another Chevrolet NASCAR in 2012. That's an average of 217 mph over a 90-mile course.

Because of the early start it meant my race was all over before nine in the morning, but plenty of other cars had to come through, so we were probably waiting three hours for them to finish. We were parked out in the middle of the desert, with nothing there but a hot-dog stand. My race boots were a bit tight, so I took them off, and I was walking around in my bare feet eating a hot dog and looking at the cars as they turned up. I got yarning to a matey-boy with a really tidy Mustang. I enjoyed talking to people, instead of them talking to me, because no one knew who I was. Considering the speeds folk were doing, and it's only amateur enthusiasts in road cars, I was dead impressed that only one car broke down out of 150-odd, and no one crashed.

I'm right into the amateur American motorsport. There's no interviews, no 'I'd like to thank the Monster.' No one's putting the right pair of sunglasses on before being photographed. No one cares. It made me think about going back to Pikes Peak with the Rob North wall of death bike, once I've stuck a supercharger on it, but I don't know if I ever will.

Half the film crew were at the start and half were at

the finish. Once they got what they needed they cleared off back to Vegas, leaving me and John to drive 20 miles south on the road, to a petrol station, where I had the first decent cup of tea I'd had since I'd been in America. Paul from Krazy Horse was with us and we were there a couple of hours, waiting for the trailer to turn up. The Transit wasn't road legal, so I didn't want to risk driving it all the way to Vegas. Eventually, Nam turned up with the car transporter and FT13 AFK was loaded up.

I had enjoyed the whole experience, but I couldn't stop thinking that I'd rather be in Dan's and James's position of working on the thing. I hadn't been about for this programme because it all clashed with the wall of death. It was still my van but it didn't mean anything like as much to me as the wall of death bike did. The lads from Krazy Horse and Radical had been working their bollocks off to sort the van out while I was tossing it off around Las Vegas on a borrowed motorbike. Then I would just go drive it. I felt like a *Top Gear* wanker or summat. I'd have much rather been doing it, then sticking someone else in it or letting me drive it. It reminded me that I don't want to be a TV presenter. I want my cake and I want to eat it.

The cost of building the van went way over budget. The TV lot had £120,000 in it and were keen to get some of that money back, so they offered to sell it to me for £30,000, but it was still the van I'd bought back from the insurance company for £900, albeit with over a hundred grand spent on it. I liked the van, but I didn't want it 30-grand badly. Then North One thought they could sell it in America, but that wasn't an option, so I told them, 'It's no use to me as it is. Just turn it back to a road van and I'll have it back,' and they said, 'Oh, you can have it, then.'

The next plan for it is to leave it in America for when I fly out to Bonneville Salt Flats to attempt the land-speed record in the Triumph streamliner, and try to break a record with it at the same time. I don't know what potential the Transit has. Radical reckon it's fit for 200 mph. I'm not convinced, but I might be wrong and there's one way to find out.

The Monday morning after the Transit race I was waiting at the hotel for the bus to the airport and had some time to kill, so I went on to the hotel computer for an hour, looking at flights to Canada for the Tour Divide, which I still hadn't sorted. The North West 200 was on when I was out in America, and I hadn't thought I should have been there, but I looked up the results and saw that Malachi Mitchell-Thomas had died and Ryan Farquhar had crashed on the TAS BMW.

Mitchell-Thomas was 20 and had won the Manx Grand Prix the previous year, the Manx being the race run on the same circuit as the Isle of Man TT, but aimed at riders of classics, amateurs on modern bikes and those looking to step up to the TT. I didn't know him, but people had good things to say about him. It was his first year racing in Ireland and he'd got permission to race at the North West. I wasn't allowed to race there in my first year, even though I'd been racing in the British National championship and had been racing the national road races in Ireland, so they must have made an exception for him because of that Manx experience.

Ryan Farquhar, the Northern Irish rider I'd raced against more than any other rider in my whole time on the roads, had a massive crash at the North West too, but survived. Reports said that he was seriously ill at the time, with a load of broken ribs and a lacerated liver. Ryan is very different to me, but I've always respected him. He'd retired a few years before, after his uncle died after a crash at the Manx in 2012. I'd written in *When You Dead, You Dead* that I was surprised he'd made a comeback and that I hoped he'd keep looking for something else to replace the buzz of racing. He was 40 when he crashed at the North West. John McGuinness and Bruce Anstey have proved you can still be right on the pace in international road races well into your forties, but if there are very good reasons that made you stop racing, and it seems like Ryan had them, then remember them. He was on the mend when I wrote this, which is great news, and so much better than it sounded in the first couple of weeks after the accident, when he was in and out of intensive care.

When I got home from America, Cammy and the Northern Irish racer he spanners for now, Lee Johnston, came round to the house. I was quizzing them like hell about their preparation for the TT, and for a while I was dead excited about road racing again. Then, a couple of minutes later, I thought, Nah! I don't need to be road racing.

CHAPTER 10

I'd been soft for too long

I'D ONLY BEEN back for a couple of weeks before I was heading to North America again for another time trial, this time a bit longer and a lot slower. The Tour Divide is called the world's toughest bicycle race and stretches from Banff in Canada to Antelope Wells on the Mexican border. The race has been described as an extreme test of endurance, self-reliance and mental toughness. And it sounded a bit of me. There are no entry fees, no prizes and no sponsors. It's purely amateur.

I was told about the race by Stu Thomson. In January 2011, I'd done the Strathpuffer, the 24-hour mountain bike race held up in the north of Scotland, and two weeks later I was out in Oman doing a different kind of mountain-bike race, a four-day stage race, the Trans Hajar. It was a lot different to what I was used to. The Trans Hajar was short days at a very fast speed, and I had to turn myself inside out to be anything like on the pace, because it was more like sprinting. I'm more like a 24-hour slogger, but I was right into it. Stu is best known for making Danny MacAskill's world famous bike-stunt videos, but he's done other stuff, including some music videos. Stu was there, wearing two hats, filming for Orange, the British mountain-bike company, and for the race organisers, the Oman government and tourist board. His film was all about the race, and because I was taking part in it, he was filming odd bits with me.

At the end of the race he told me to let him know if I ever wanted to film anything with him. I said if he came up with some oddball ideas or something that had a good chance of breaking me then I'd probably be up for it.

A while later he rang me and said, 'Right, I've found something. There's a mountain-bike race in America, the longest in the world, this many miles, got this much climbing. It's called the Tour Divide.' That was the first I'd heard of it, and I liked the sound of it. We didn't speak about it a lot, just odd bits, but it was a fair topic for a year. We'd talk on the phone every couple of months, and he sent me a couple of videos, but I soon realised it was the same time as the Isle of Man TT, and that meant I wasn't going to be able to do it for a while, because the TT was the middle of the racing year. Even if I wasn't enjoying it as much as I used to, everything before the TT was building up to it, everything after was the slowdown. I was in that rut. While the TT wasn't the be-all and end-all, like it had been for me in 2006, 2007 and 2008, it was still important. But the seed had been planted, and I loved the sound of the Tour Divide.

I was enjoying the Isle of Man TT less and less every year. It seemed like it was getting buried under more people, more bullshit, more mither. I still loved the racing, but it felt like it was harder to dig down to that through everything else. I enjoyed the 2015 TT, because I stayed out of the way and I had the dog out there with me, but I still drove home after the fortnight was over thinking, What am I doing? I wasn't there to make up the numbers. I'd gone faster than I ever had before, with a 132.398 mph lap in the 2015 Senior, and on the podium in the 600 race. So I was licking on, but I'd probably rather have been at work. There were good bits. I got to ride my bike around the TT course and walk my dog in the hills and go pushbiking, but I was going through the motions. I'd done it for years, and even though it's the Isle of Man TT, it's still only a motorbike race.

The rest of the year was more of the same. I did some Irish national races, the Southern 100 and then the Ulster Grand Prix, where I spannered myself. While I was in that Belfast hospital for a week, I thought, I know what, I'm going to do that mountain-bike race next year. The decision was made as I lay there, bollocksed. It might have been because I knew I could, very easily, have been stuck in a bed paralysed, waiting to be spoon-fed my next meal. It was a big crash and I'd broken my back again, so it didn't take a great deal of imagination to wonder what might have been.

I went back to work and started telling people that I was going to miss the TT, to do this mountain-bike race. Most people thought it was a good idea. I told Philip Neill, the boss of the TAS racing team I'd been with since 2011, so he could look for someone to replace me. By the end of the year, I knew that it would take so much to get ready for the Tour Divide that I didn't want to risk getting an injury racing a motorbike in the build-up. If I broke or even twisted something it would knacker my training up. From the Ulster in August 2015, to June 2016, I hadn't raced a motorbike, but I wasn't missing them, because I was still doing plenty with them, especially with the wall of death. It was different to racing, but that wasn't a bad thing, and training for the Tour Divide was taking up every bit of spare time and thought.

I spoke to Stu Thomson and Jason Miles about making a programme about the Tour Divide, but in the end it didn't feel like the right thing to do. I reckoned that filming and becoming more recognisable from the TV stuff had buggered up my enjoyment of being at motorcycle races, and I didn't want to risk the same happening with bicycle races. I like it just as it is. It's my thing. And now, looking back, I'm pleased I didn't go along with the idea of filming it.

So, by Sunday afternoon, 5 June, the training was finished and I couldn't do any more. I had bought and modified a bike for the job with help from a mate, because I was busy with the wall of death bike. I was booked on a flight to Calgary, Canada, with the return flight from Phoenix, Arizona, a couple of thousand miles away.

I'd spent the Friday before sorting the last few bits, and I had nothing left to do on Saturday. I was sorted. The bike was packed, everything was done. Jon from Louth Cycle Centre had originally built the bike and I'd got it back to mine and done a few things. If it wasn't for him, I'd have converted one of my 24-hour race bikes for it, but he had the proper thing, a Salsa Fargo. It's a cheap bike, about £800 or summat, but the bloke who held the Tour Divide record, Josh Kato, used the same Fargo frame when he set his record time. We upgraded a load of stuff, though, fitting some suspension forks, a Rohloff hub in the back and a dead fancy dynamo front hub to power the lights and recharge my satnav. This Salsa had been in John's shop for years. It's a bit of a strange bike – it's neither a road bike nor a mountain bike, but it has mountain-bike tyres.

When the day arrived, Sharon took me to the airport in the Transit. I lifted the bike out of the van then said, 'See ya, lass.' I'm not one for big, emotional goodbyes. I'd see her in three weeks in New Mexico, all being well.

I flew out economy class. I was thinking about upgrading, but I didn't ask the price, so it never got to more than thinking. You still get to the same place at the same time, however much you pay.

I landed in Calgary at nine or ten at night, got my bike on a trolley and just had my Kriega backpack with my riding shoes and helmet in it on my back – that was it as far as luggage. I was wearing some knackered old trainers, because I knew I would have to leave them. I wasn't going to carry anything I didn't need to.

Now it was me, myself and I, alone, and I began to realise that the racing and the TV work has made me soft. There was no one telling me, 'Right you need to be here at this time, you need to be there at that time,' like

I'd got used to. Even the Pikes Peak and the Transit jobs were like that. There's a bit of work on my part, but it's all organised. For the last eight or nine years, since I left Team Racing and joined AIM Yamaha, even when I went racing I'd go and sign on, and then the bikes, tyres and fuel were all sorted. I just had to ride the things. When I was building the wall of death bike I had to organise and make a load of bits, and go on a course to learn how to CNC program, but it was only bits, not the whole job. This was different, though. The Tour Divide was all on me. I had to get all the way down the Continental Divide to Mexico, not really knowing owt except the bits I'd read in books and watched in a documentary.

The last bit that had been sorted for me was a nice hotel in Banff, the mountain holiday-resort town the race starts from. Spellman had booked that. I checked in late Sunday, early Monday morning after getting the bus for the two-hour journey from Calgary airport. The next day I bolted the bike together, as it had been partially stripped to fit in the special travel bag. It was packed with all the specialist luggage strapped to it, and everything I thought I'd need already in the bags. Next I started on the list of jobs I'd written for myself. I had to get some salt tablets, energy bars and a pair of short, lightweight socks. I had travelled out in winter ones, but my feet were sweltering on the plane, and it got me thinking about the deserts I had to ride through, so I reckoned I needed an option.

I didn't have to sign on with anyone because there's no one at the start and no one at the finish. It's an underground race and they want to keep it that way. I don't think they would take kindly to people going and filming it (though they filmed it in the past to help get it off the ground), so that was another good reason for us not to. There's no reception for the racers, no welcome packs, nothing. All you do is go online to register your SPOT Tracker the day before you plan to set off, and that tells the organisers where you are and how long it's taking you.

The SPOT Tracker is about half the size of a smartphone. It has an orange rubber casing to survive a few hard drops. It's a device that can track your route and send messages to pre-set numbers or addresses. It doesn't rely on mobile phone networks, it operates purely by satellite, so as long as it can see the sky it can send a message. All sorts of folk use them: mountaineers, off-road motorcyclists, hikers, light-aircraft pilots. The SPOT Tracker doesn't have a screen, just a few buttons. One has a small hand reaching for a bigger hand, which sends a signal saying, 'I'm in trouble, but I'll sort it out.' You have to lift a rubber flap to get to it, so you can't push it by mistake.

There's another button, with SOS on it, and if you press that you're telling the emergency services, 'I'm fucked!'

and they send GEOS global rescue to come and get you wherever you are in the world. Then send you the bill. When I signed up there were only six places in the world that the GEOS rescue folk wouldn't cover – Afghanistan, Chechnya, Democratic Republic of Congo, Iraq, Somalia and Israel. I'd be well off course if I found myself in any of them when I was thinking about pressing the button.

There's a speech-bubble button that sends a pre-set message to up to five numbers that you put in there, but you had to pay extra for it, so I didn't bother. You have to pay a year's subscription, but you can choose different levels of coverage and I got the lowest one, so not all the buttons on my SPOT Tracker did owt. There's a button with a tick that sends a confirmation whenever I press it, to say, I'm OK. I sent that to Sharon, my sister Sally and my mate Dobby. I don't really know why Dobby, but he wanted to know and he's a good mate.

The other important button has a shoe print on it. You press that when you first set off and it starts the SPOT Tracker sending a signal every ten minutes, tracking your speed and position on a map, without you doing anything. That's what they use to put you on the map on the Trackleaders website. All I had to do was keep it charged up and not lose it.

Banff didn't look like it was full of dead-fit athletes, but I think that's because I arrived early and anyone else taking part hadn't got there yet. There was one bloke in my hotel who was sat on his own as well, legs shaved, head shaved, lean as hell. I heard him talk to someone and he was British, but I didn't try to make conversation with him. I like my own company and I knew I was up to the job, so I didn't need to speak to anyone to suss the landscape.

Because of the way the cheap flights I'd booked worked, I flew out on 5 June and I was supposed to fly back on 29 June. I felt I'd done everything I could with the training, but I knew that not many folk had completed the ride in under 20 days – fewer than 50 in total – and it was already at the back of my mind that I didn't want to miss the flight home. Sharon had got hold of Matthew Lee. He is one of the most experienced riders, and he sets the route and gives people advice. He's just a brilliant bloke. Matthew was featured in a film of the 2008 Tour Divide I'd watched, called *Ride the Divide*. He had held the record for the course, setting it at 19 days, 12 hours in 2008. He broke his own record in 2009 and improved on it again in 2010, lowering it to 17 days, 16 hours and 10 minutes. Since then it had been broken in 2011, 2013 and 2015, with Josh Kato, from Washington State, holding the outright record at 14 days, 11 hours and 27 minutes going into the 2016 race. Bethany Dunne has the best ever women's time at 19 days, 2 hours and 37 minutes, nearly 10 hours quicker than Matthew's record time in 2008.

Friday 10 June would be the Grand Départ for the 2016 Tour Divide, the Grand Départ being the name for the official group start they use in the Tour de France. I was told that the British weekly motorbike paper *Motorcycle News* had contacted the organisers to find out when I was leaving and work out who could interview me and take photos at the start, and I didn't want anything like that. I also couldn't understand what me taking part in a bicycle race in North America had to do with motorbikes and *MCN*, so I entered and registered my SPOT Tracker under the pseudonym Terry Smith.

Sharon explained to Matthew Lee that I wasn't bothered about being part of the race – I just wanted to know how long it would take me to do the ride – and he emailed back saying I could set off at any time between June and September and my time would count, but I wouldn't get a finishing position in the race if I didn't leave with the Grand Départ. I wasn't bothered about that. I just wanted a time for myself, and to know I could do it.

So even before I left England, I told Sharon and Spellman that I was going to set off earlier in the week. I thought Wednesday morning would be best, giving me the chance to get over the flight and have a couple of good nights' rest before leaving, but by Monday afternoon I'd done nearly everything I needed to in Banff, and as beautiful a place as it is, I was itching to go. I could have sat there, drinking posh coffee for a few more days, but I couldn't settle.

On Monday afternoon I biked up to where the race would start from, the beginning of the Spray River West trail. It was no distance out of town, but it still took a bit of finding. I thought there might be something to tell me that this was the start of the Tour Divide route, but there was nothing. There was just a regular kind of wooden sign for the trail and a noticeboard with glazed doors on it, like you might have outside a village hall or a church. I knew it was the right place, though, I'd put the route in my Garmin GPS unit and it confirmed I was at the start, and also that I was 4,500 feet above sea level.

There was an old boy, in his sixties, out for a ride on his bike. He asked, 'Are you doing the Tour Divide race?' I told him I was, and he said, 'That's a big job, that,' before explaining that he was a physical trainer. I told him that I wanted to stay out of the way of all the bother and I was going to leave on Wednesday. He said, 'Why don't you set off tomorrow?' And I thought, Yeah, why don't I?

On my way back to the hotel I pedalled to the post office to find out how much it would cost to send the brand new bike bag back, and they told me $400. The bag was good, but not that good, so I left it with the lass at the post office and had her promise me it would go to a good home. I could have sent my bike out in an old bag but it was important that it arrived in one piece. I'd got a really good bag to protect the bike, and it broke my heart to leave the brand new luggage behind.

I asked a passer-by if they knew anywhere to get my hair cut and they pointed me around the corner. The lass who cut it was real cool, red hair, loads of tattoos. She reckoned she'd only just started talking English, because she'd moved from Quebec, the French-talking part of Canada. There was a lot of hair to get rid of, so I just asked her to lob it off. I told her what I was up to, but I wasn't making a big deal of it and I'm not sure she grasped what I was doing.

That night I had a big feed of steak and salad in the hotel, then went to the bar and had a couple of pints. I like sitting in bars on my own. I reckon if I was in a bar with someone and saw a bloke sat alone I'd think he was a bit strange, but I like it. I was weighing the job up, knowing it was the biggest thing I'd ever undertaken. I'd done a fair bit of reading on the subject and plenty of training, but it was still a ride into the unknown. And I liked that about it too.

It'd have been about ten o'clock on Monday night by the time I'd supped up. The hotel computer was downstairs, next to the Coke machine. I went on to the Trackleaders website and put in my start time, nine o'clock Tuesday morning. Now I was registered, the organisers, and anyone else who was interested, could follow my progress at any time.

I wanted to catch up on sleep before I set off, but I woke up early on Tuesday, before six. I couldn't sleep. Nothing had made me nervous like this for years. I'd done three-day rides. I'd done quite a lot of tough 24-hour stuff. But not 2,745 miles. Sharon was confident I could do it, so was Dobby, Spellman and a few other mates, but there was still doubt in my own mind.

I folded up the T-shirt I'd flown out in and left it on top of the old trainers I was leaving behind. Even after loads of breakfast I was still ready to go at half-seven. I rode to the start, 15 minutes away from the hotel, waited until exactly eight on my Garmin and set off. It didn't matter that I'd said I was leaving at nine, because the SPOT Tracker would pick up on it.

It was a beautiful day as I pedalled off on the first mile, thinking, Only 2,745 of these to go. I like looking at things in fractions. Soon I was a thousandth of the way through it. I never thought, Oh, I can do this. I had read that I had to take every day as it comes. Even the fittest folk get injuries that stop them completing the race.

I found it a bit difficult to pace myself on the first day. The temperature felt in the mid-20s and it was perfect biking weather. I was ten hours in and thought I was doing alright. I had one book with me, *Cycling the Great Divide: From Canada to Mexico on North America's Premier Long-Distance Mountain Bike Route* by Michael McCoy. It's aimed at touring cyclists, not the

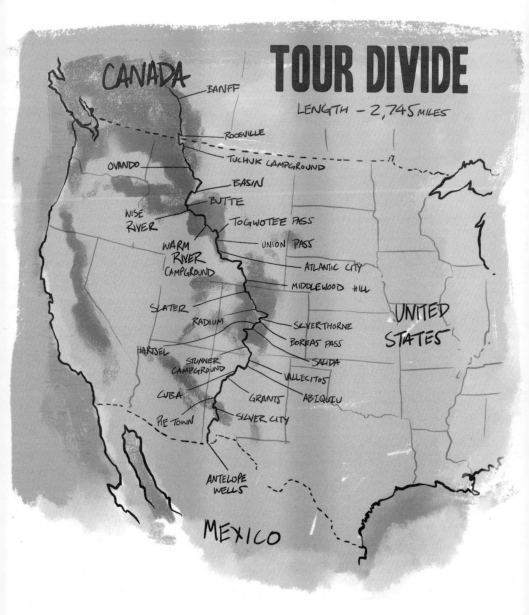

more hardcore Tour Divide riders, but the information crosses over. It has detailed maps of the trails and day-by-day breakdowns of what to expect, where to get food and where to camp, but because it's aimed at tourists enjoying themselves, not masochists trying to break themselves, the route is spread over 70 days. I still wanted to do it in less than 20. And I had to do it in under 22 days if I didn't want to miss my flight.

From everything I'd read about the race I knew that if I got to Butts Cabin, which is about 180 miles in, on the first night, I was doing alright, and I reckoned I might get there. I was cycling in absolutely beautiful countryside, past Spray Lakes Reservoir and Canyon Dam. I made my first crossing of the Continental Divide, which gives the route and the race its name.

The Continental Divide is the crooked line running through North America that divides the continent into two drainage areas. It runs from Alaska, through Canada, mainland USA and into Mexico and beyond. On one side all the rivers run to the Atlantic Ocean (or the Gulf of Mexico), and on the other they run to the Pacific. The Continental Divide follows the Rocky Mountains, which was why I, and all the other Tour Divide riders, had the equivalent of seven Everests' worth of climbing between Banff and Antelope Wells.

I climbed up to 6,443 feet at Elk Pass and followed the Elk River. I went through the town of Sparwood,

British Columbia. If I had been following the suggested daily mileages in my guidebook, I'd have been at the end of day five already, but I hadn't even stopped to eat. I changed that in Sparwood, pulling up at a petrol station with a shop attached to it and loading up with cinnamon rolls, doughnuts, full-fat milk and Gatorade.

I was following my Garmin, and the trail was fairly obvious a lot of the time, but because I hadn't downloaded the USA map background on to my device it just showed a line, and me as a dot on it. It didn't show any other references like lakes, rivers or mountains, so it wasn't always totally clear. The whole route was marked out using 10,000 waypoints, so at times the detail wasn't that fine, but I'd thought I'd be alright. I should've spent the money on the US map to load into it.

I knew that I shouldn't ride until I couldn't pedal any more before deciding to stop for the night. I was only 20 miles, if that, from Butts Cabin, and anyone who is going to do the winning is always at Butts Cabin on the first night. But by that point I was thinking to myself that I was in such a beautiful country, and I'd already seen so much memorable stuff, that I was just going to ride the Tour Divide and not race it. I wouldn't hang about, but I wouldn't kill myself to try to get close to a record time.

I stopped at 11 o'clock at the end of the first day. I'd covered 165 miles, about 16 per cent of the overall route, and it had been an easy enough day to start off with.

There had been a little bit of tarmac road, but it was mainly off-road on broad gravel tracks with plenty of climbing, much more than I was used to. There had been nothing daft and I was averaging 13 to 14 mph, which was some going for a bike that weighed 25 kilograms with all my kit on it.

Day one was over and I was loving it. I'd been soft for too long. Nothing was going to be soft for the next 18 days.

CHAPTER 11

Locking the door to keep the bears out

I LAY DOWN at the side of the trail, on the Flathead Pass, for the first night's rest of my Tour Divide. The altitude of the pass is 5,900 feet, which was bugger all compared to some of the passes and summits I was going to cycle over, but there are 5,280 feet in a mile so I was well over a mile above sea level. As a comparison, the summit of Britain's highest mountain, Ben Nevis, is 4,406 feet.

The guidebook said I was on the Grizzly Bear Highway, in an area of Canada that has 'the largest population of inland grizzlies on the North American Continent'. Those in the know say to make as much noise as possible so you don't sneak up on the furry fellas and startle them. Cougars, wolves, and all the deer, elk and moose, which the carnivores eat, call this area home, too.

The closest I got to a bear was something like ten metres, when a young 'un walked across the trail in front of me on the Richmond Pass, in Montana. That's when you're most at risk, because the mothers will do anything to protect their cubs if they feel threatened or frightened. When I saw the cub, I tensed up, wondering what was following, so I reached around to my rucksack, grabbed my whistle and blew like hell.

I also saw moose, wild horses, wild dogs, skunks, raccoons and loads of pronghorns. They're like deer that spring on all fours to get around. I must have seen a thousand of them.

The book also said that I was in the last major valley in southern Canada to be completely uninhabited. The Tour Divide used to take a different route, through more towns and on more tarmac, but it was changed to this wilder one. As I went to sleep every night, the whistle and bear spray that Sharon had bought me from

GO Outdoors was right next to my head. The thought of being eaten in my sleep wasn't enough to keep me awake, and I slept until the alarm went off at 3.30. It was still dark, but I had my head torch on while I packed all my sleeping stuff back on the bike. I was ready to go at 4.30, and I was about 90 miles from the border with America.

Within only a few miles the bike path had been washed away by a landslide, so I had to scramble down the loose rocks and wade along the river. Next was a 12-mile climb past Butts Cabin over Cabin Pass, then up a tough-as-hell slog over Galton Pass. There was snow on the top and it pissed it down. My muscles felt OK, but I had a slight twinge in my left Achilles. It wasn't a problem, but I could feel it, and I was hoping it wouldn't develop into anything.

The descent was fast as hell: rough, wild and a full 3,000 feet to the border crossing at Roosville. I was there before midday and wet through. The rain and snow hadn't bothered me, though. Biking to work in Grimsby through the winter had stood me in good stead.

When I reached the American border, the customs officer told me I had the wrong visa. I had a work visa, and he asked, 'Are you working?' He wasn't the chattiest. I said I was riding my bike. I could've told him I was researching this book, but I wasn't thinking. I had to buy a tourist visa and it only cost $6, but still …

Now I was in Montana, biking the ten miles to Eureka where I filled my face in a Subway, the first food I hadn't carried myself since breakfast in Banff, over 260 miles ago. I didn't go looking for the Subway, but I was in there without a second thought.

Out of Eureka it really began to dawn on me that, even though I was heading south, as the crow flies, the trails were so winding that I was heading north for decent stretches.

It was beautiful out there and I loved riding my bike so much, on my own, just the crunch of tyres on the gravel, that I'd keep plugging away until it got dark. I'd have an idea of where I wanted to get to, and as it got closer to 11 o'clock I'd start thinking harder about it. But you can't take anything for granted on the Tour Divide. It's a tough route, hard on the body and bike. Earlier in the day the bearings in my pedal collapsed, and the part of the pedal that was clipped to my shoe came off the spindle that was fastened to the crank arm. All that was left was a metal spindle smaller than your little finger. There was no way of fixing it, but, if I was lucky, I could line up the remains of the pedal on my shoe with the spindle, and that made it a bit easier, but it wasn't right. And I was soaked to the skin.

Later that night I was pedalling down a mountain pass in the dark when my pedal shot off for the second time and I lost the part that clipped to my shoe. Oh, bloody hell. It was God knows how many miles to the next town, where there might not even be a bike shop. These clip-in pedals, designed to fasten to special cycling shoes, are only the size of a Ritz Cracker. I must have spent an hour scanning down the slopes with my head torch trying to find a bit of pedal to help me get by. It was only the end of the second day. I didn't know if my ankle being slightly out of line, and full of metalwork, was causing the bearings in my pedals to wear quicker, but I had tried to account for it with the angle of the clip on my shoe. I must have been doing something wrong, as it should've lasted longer than this. So now I had one good pedal and one slippery plastic sole trying, and failing, to grip on a finger of polished metal.

I'd read that this area was so remote that the wildlife folk who deal with such things relocate the hooligan grizzly bears – the ones that are too antisocial to live anywhere else – out here. I'd forgotten about this by the time I thought it would be the perfect place for my second night's rest stop.

I slept in campsite bogs at Tuchuk Campground, locking the door to keep the bears out. I got there late, so I didn't bother paying, and the campsite was deserted anyway. The loo was in a wooden cabin shed and it was a proper porcelain toilet, but you shat straight into a septic tank, not a sewer system. It didn't stink, or if it did I couldn't catch a whiff of it with my bad sense of smell,

Paul from Krazy Horse with an Elvis impersonator on Fremont Street, Las Vegas.

You see Mustangs if not every day, then a lot, but the attention to detail on this one was something else.

FT13 AFK at the Radical Ventures garage in Vegas. They helped us out loads when we had to fit a new clutch.

The rally computer that my navigator used is on the passenger side. In the middle is the tyre-temperature gauge. The dash is the same as the one I have in the Volvo and in the land speed record Triumph.

Busy: 3.5-litre, V6 twin turbo.

The rear wing is a work of art, designed by Wirth Research for an LMP2 (Le Mans Prototype) car.

Dan from Krazy Horse, who built the
van. Don't know why he's biting his
nails – what could possibly go wrong?

A right rare John Deere that I saw when I
went out for a pushbike ride in Nevada.

The poster for the Hookers' Choice award
before the Nevada Open Road Challenge.
The Transit won.

My bike leaning against the official start of the Tour Divide. There's a bicycle pump and a multitool attached to the sign for people to use in an emergency. You don't see that in Britain.

COLD DRINKS
ESPRESSO
ICE CREAM
SNACKS
LODGING

Just after I stopped here, in Ovando, it started heshing it down, so I camped out in a wigwam and then moved to a covered wagon when the wigwam leaked. That was my shortest day of the Tour Divide.

Mick the Paddy, a lucky charm Sharon gave me that I carried on the Tour Divide.

This is fairly early on. Only about 5 per cent of the whole 2,745-mile route was on road like this.

Home-cooked grub near Butte, I think.

These are all at the top of Togwotee Pass. I slept in someone's log shed for an hour near here.

The Basin, on the border of Montana and Wyoming. This was the day I missed Atlantic City so had to do without supplies, and I rode for well over a hundred miles with no food and not much water until I got to Wamsutter.

One of the nodding donkey oil pumps out in the desert.

Supply stop in Columbine, Colorado. I liked places like this, friendly and different, but they didn't have the range of supplies the petrol stations had. They wouldn't take my card and I was out of money, so I had to pay in Canadian dollars.

but it was warm in there. I don't know if that's to do with the chemical reaction of the shite decomposing. I was soaking wet so I was just happy for a bit of warmth. The lights were on in the bog all night and I couldn't sleep, so I put my head torch on, found the master switch outside and flicked it off, then went back in, locked the door and got my head down.

I set my alarm for 3.30 most mornings, and this one was no different. My pedal was still knackered, so I went over Whitefish Divide without a bloody pedal, which made it feel a lot harder than it should have. The surface was mainly gravel, with some tarmac early on. It was steep in places, and there were times, in the valleys, when I was nearly deafened by nearby running water. It didn't help that I went ten miles in the wrong direction.

I got over the top of the 5,300-foot pass and into Whitefish, and went looking for a bike shop. In the end I'd had to ride over 75 miles with a broken right pedal. I found a bike shop, the Glacier Cyclery, that had everything I needed. I found out later that it had been voted one of the best bike shops in America. There was a bloke outside the shop, another customer, and it turned out that he knew my mate Gary, and he knew all about Dirt Quake. He was a cool dude, a motorcycle journalist or worked in magazines or summat, and he knew who I was. He was riding east to west on mountain-bike trails, with me heading north to south, and we meet at that exact moment. It was a coincidence, but then I know a lot of people who know a lot of people.

I was travelling so light that I had to borrow a tool to change the pedals from the shop. The Glacier Cyclery was ready for the Tour Divide and knew that the leaders of the race would be coming through on Sunday and Monday, so they were going to stay open.

I bought some Crankbrothers pedals, the same as the ones I set off with, and some fingerless gloves. I'd only packed winter gloves, because I thought I was hard and I didn't need anything on my hands for padding except when it got freezing, but I was wrong. The trails were so rough my hands were getting a battering. Usually, I ride with just the heel of my hand on the bars, not my fingers wrapped around the grip. My hands can put up with a lot, but that part of my palm was already sore and beginning to blister, after only two days, and I'd had to change my riding position to compensate for it. I bought some energy bars too, packed up, filled my face and set off.

Before Whitefish the going was very mountainous and forested, but it flattened out after it for 30-odd miles, though I messed up and rode ten miles out of my way. There were two trails next to each other, and I thought I was on the correct one. It looked like I was on the right route on the Garmin screen too, but the trails started separating and I realised I was on the wrong path and had to double back.

The next decent-sized place was Ferndale. I stopped for pizza and a tub of ice cream. I sat outside, on a red-hot early evening, thinking, This is it, this is ace. The bloke from the shop came out for a fag, and we had a yarn. He asked where I was going and I told him Mexico. He started telling me about his life, how he'd moved a bit out of town because it was cheaper. He went back in the shop and came out with a yellow beer cooler – I think they call them a coozie, a little foam rubber jacket you slip your can or bottle in to keep it cold. It had the shop's name, Ferndale Market, printed on it. He wished me luck and I kept hold of the cooler, but I didn't know when I'd ever use it. I didn't take a spare pair of socks because I was thinking about every ounce of weight, but I carried that all the way.

I used to think Americans were very American, and that everything was a willy-waving contest: What do you do for a living? What car have you got? Trying to put you in a box before they've hardly met you. But this trip totally changed my opinion. Americans are the politest, nicest people. Before this, one of the few sniffs I'd got of Americans not being the kind of people I'd pigeonholed them as was when I went to Portland in 2015 to meet Matt Markstaller to discuss the Triumph land speed record attempt. That was the first time I'd seen real America, not tourist America. A few folk at Pikes Peak were on a wavelength too, but it was at a race so there was some willy-waving. Even when I went on a ten-day road trip in a rented camper van with my mates, when we were all in our mid-twenties, driving from Los Angeles to San Francisco and then to Las Vegas, it was all very touristy with the kind of people that confirmed the stereotype I had of them.

Out of Ferndale I was riding along the side of Swan Lake and then the little rivers that are called creeks out here. I was near Fatty Creek, at ten at night, when I called it a day. I slept out on a bit of flat ground in the wilderness. I didn't have a tent, but I had my self-inflating roll mat, which was only about an inch thick but gave good insulation from the cold ground and provided a bit of padding. I climbed into my sleeping bag and bivvy bag, which goes over the sleeping bag as an extra layer of insulation.

That night the roll mat got punctured by a stone and was useless. I ended up carrying it for a couple of more days, thinking it would at least do something, even if it wasn't giving any padding, but then I chucked it. I had at least two weeks of sleeping rough to go, and I didn't even have a roll mat any more.

The coldest parts of the whole Tour Divide were the Montana mountain passes. At some points the snow was piled 10-foot high at the side of the trails.

I'd thought dead hard about how to pack the bike for the trip. All the luggage I had was made by a company called Apidura. The bag under my handlebars held my sleeping department: roll mat (until I punctured it), sleeping bag, bivvy bag and woolly hat, which I slept in so I didn't lose all my body heat out of my head. This pack had an elasticated string pocket on the back, so it also became the food department, where I stored my cinnamon buns, doughnuts, protein bodybuilder bars or apple pies – anything I could buy at each stop.

The Garmin GPS and lights were fastened to the bars. I had 'tri' bars – triathlon bars – which are long, forward-facing add-ons. They bolt either side of the steering stem and have cups for your elbows, so when you hold on to the bars you get into a more aerodynamic position, with your hands stretched ahead of you, back curved and head low. I didn't fit them to be more aerodynamic, but just so I had different riding positions. If I had an ache, I could move my body into a different position to try to ease it.

My head torch stretched over the bars. The front-wheel dynamo would charge anything with a USB socket, which included my Garmin, lights, SPOT Tracker and head torch.

A little, soft bag hung from the bars, with all the stuff I needed quick access to: sun cream, sunglasses, salt tablets for my drinks, water-purification tablets and mosquito spray.

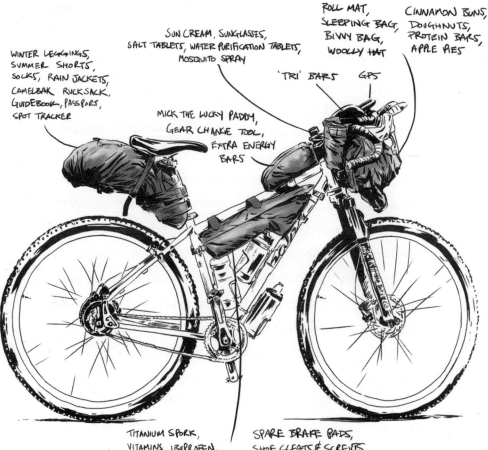

WINTER LEGGINGS,
SUMMER SHORTS,
SOCKS, RAIN JACKETS,
CAMELBAK RUCKSACK,
GUIDEBOOK, PASSPORT,
SPOT TRACKER

SUN CREAM, SUNGLASSES,
SALT TABLETS, WATER PURIFICATION TABLETS,
MOSQUITO SPRAY

ROLL MAT,
SLEEPING BAG,
BIVVY BAG,
WOOLLY HAT

CINNAMON BUNS,
DOUGHNUTS,
PROTEIN BARS,
APPLE PIES

MICK THE LUCKY PADDY,
GEAR CHANGE TOOL,
EXTRA ENERGY
BARS

'TRI' BARS   GPS

TITANIUM SPORK,
VITAMINS, IBUPROFEN,
WATER PURIFICATION TABLETS,
DIARRHOEA TABLETS,
ELASTIC BANDS, CABLE TIES

SPARE BRAKE PADS,
SHOE CLEATS & SCREWS,
CHAIN, GEAR CABLES, OIL,
CHAIN TOOLS, SWISS ARMY KNIFE

There was a small top-tube pack at the stem, which had in there Mick the lucky paddy that Sharon had given me as a good-luck charm, and a tool that allowed me to change gear when the gear shifter stopped working, but I'll come to that later. I'd put more energy bars in there, when I had them. Petrol stations sold them – Clif bars, MET-Rx bars, owt like that.

In the triangle of the frame, hung from the top tube, I had another narrow bag. It was split down the middle, and the right section was packed with spare brake pads, shoe cleats and shoe-cleat screws, and a chain; gear cables, inners and outers; chain oil; chain tools, and a Swiss army knife. I would end up going through three sets of brake pads and three sets of shoe cleats on the Tour Divide.

On the left-hand side I had my titanium spork – knife, fork and spoon, all in one, which I used for eating big pots of fruit that I bought from petrol stations – and vitamins and ibuprofen. I ate all the vitamins, but I didn't take one painkiller. I had more water-purification tablets, diarrhoea tablets – which I didn't use – elastic bands – useful for fastening stuff that broke to the bike – and cable ties.

The final pack was under my seat. In there were my winter leggings or summer shorts, depending on which I was wearing, and summer or winter socks, again, depending which I had on. I had a proper cycling rain jacket, which I needed every morning, and a really lightweight rain jacket that I didn't sweat too much in, to use during the day to stop me getting sunburnt. The winter leggings had better arse padding, so about a week from the end, when I got near New Mexico, I made them into shorts with my Swiss army knife, so I could wear them in the heat. I also had my CamelBak rucksack that had the guidebook and passport in it, and SPOT Tracker attached to it.

The bike frame had three bottle cages, but the big bottle in the bottom one just held bodybuilder protein powder that I'd mix into my water to help me recover a bit overnight. I never bought bottled water, but I'd put the purification tablets in everything, even if I filled up from a tap, otherwise it tasted like a swimming pool. At the end of every day, if I had the opportunity, I'd buy full-fat milk. That was me – everything I needed for 20 days on the road.

On day four I rode past Holland Lake, which was so beautiful I stopped to take photos. There's a waterfall, a river overlooking Richmond Pass and a posh place where folk go to get married. They had a shop and a bar with a choice of fancy beers and comfy settees. It was mint, but not hard to pull myself away from it to get back on my bike. I wasn't racing – I wasn't clock-watching if my food took ten minutes to arrive. I was enjoying the whole experience, the views, the riding, the challenge of it and the people-watching.

Out of Holland Lake there were a couple of climbs that I didn't find difficult, then I found myself on a tough old road. This was a road as in a horse and cart track, not a B-road. Then I went through Grizzly Basin, a place supposed to be thick with the things, which was where I saw the cub.

I stopped in Ovando and found somewhere to eat, where I met a bloke with a black Labrador called Convoy. It was only seven o'clock at night, but I could see rain was coming in. I'd spotted a wigwam and a cowboy-film-type covered wagon that riders could sleep in and leave a donation. I thought I could either set off in the rain or bed down early and get up at 11pm to start out again, hopefully after the rain had passed. I decided to try to sit out the rain, and that meant day four was my shortest mileage day of the whole trip.

If I'd hung around and set off in the Grand Départ on Friday, I might have got to somewhere like Ovando and found that the wigwam was full, or the tiny backwoods shops I was relying on had been cleared out of the good stuff by the locust-like cyclists buying up and eating everything they could lay their hands on. That was another benefit of setting off early. The downside was that I had no wheel tracks to follow, so I was going off route and getting lost every now and then, and spending time working out which trail was the one I should be on.

The wigwam seemed the best bet, but the rain dripping

in on me woke me up, so I moved to the wagon. It was miserable being wet and going to bed. I wasn't cold when I went to sleep, because I'd been cycling, but as everything cooled and condensed in the sleeping bag, which was made even worse in the bivvy bag, I'd wake up shivering some mornings. That was one of the longest sleeps I had on the whole trip, way past the 11pm I planned, but I was still on the road at 3.30 in the morning.

The route was at a high altitude, day after day. I never felt light-headed, but it was affecting my pace. Just before the sun came up was the coldest. My water was freezing in my bottles some days, and I kept having nosebleeds. I had about 20, so one a day, on average, and they were as bad at the beginning as they were at the end of the ride. It must have been the dust and breathing hard for hour after hour. I'd blow my nose and they'd start, blood dripping out all over my Garmin and my bags, which was a pain because it would dry so quickly in the heat, and it's difficult stuff to get off.

Navigating the big and small stuff meant I had to concentrate a lot of the time, and I was riding with my head up, not head down, grinding along, following a white line like I would on the way to work. There was so much coming at me, changes of direction, tree branches that you had to pick a line to get through. I had big black scabs all over my arms from being whipped by branches and burnt trees going down Richmond Pass in the dark.

I was cycling through and near areas called Bob Marshall Wilderness and Scapegoat Wilderness, national forests and national parks. When I saw a shop or a town I would always stop to eat. I wasn't craving anything in particular or missing anything, I just wanted the most calories I could get in me. I stopped for a good omelette in Lincoln at half-seven.

A lot of the routes were cattle tracks. The climb up South Fork was brutal, with streams to cross. The word Gulch is used loads in the names. It means a ravine, usually that a river rushes down. The guidebook was really detailed, giving all the names, but there weren't many signposts to give me a clue whether I was on Lost Horse Road or Wigwam Road, or whatever. The guidebook was filling up with notes I was writing in it. I scribbled a line pointing to Lava Mountain and just wrote, Tough as fuck, 4x4 truck. This climb was steep and rutted. It must have been an off-road course for 4x4s, and I had no choice but to get off and push for two hours. The thought, This isn't much fun, never entered my head, though. I was just putting one foot in front of the other. I wasn't having negative thoughts, just, The top will come.

If you add it all up, there is more descending than climbing in the 2,700-odd miles, because Banff is at a higher altitude than Antelope Wells on the Mexican border, but it didn't feel like it. It didn't feel like it at all.

I rode into the town of Basin one night at about nine. All there was to the place was about ten houses and a pizza shop. I stuck my head into the restaurant and said, 'I'm a bit mucky, am I alright to come in for some food?' This lass who worked there said, 'You're in Basin, Montana!' As if to say, 'Who gives a fuck if you're covered in dirt?' I had a 12-inch pizza and a beer. I was drinking beer, when I could get it, because it's good for calories.

As soon as I stopped and sat down, I'd pull out the guidebook and notes, which Sharon had written out in a waterproof notepad, to see what was coming next and how far I had to the next food stop. I'd given up wondering about what percentage of the ride I'd done or how long I had left. I'd turned very machine-like. I didn't want to hang around chatting too much. Eat, ride, sleep, repeat. After the pizza and beer, I was back on the bike for a couple of hours before dossing down for the night.

Day six: I was on the road at 4.30am and had coffee and Snickers in Butte, the birthplace of Evel Knievel. Somehow, I was burning through over $100 a day in food and drink. I spent $2,000 in 18 days. I wasn't going to fancy places, but I was eating a lot. When I found a shop or petrol station I walked up to the till with four Clif bars and four MET-Rx protein bars; Muscle Milk, which is milk with added protein; regular full-fat milk; Gatorade. And that was just for starters. Then I'd have a foot-long chicken sub, piled high with salad, but no spicy stuff, and a tub of salad with more chicken, and two big cookies. Before I set off I'd go back to the service station for more milk, more energy bars and sugary, fatty shit. I would have at least two of these stops a day.

I've never had a credit card, but I carried a debit card, and it never got refused until I tried to pay for a hotel the night before I flew home. I'd go to a cash machine and take out $100 to pay for food with cash. I didn't want to risk taking more than that out, because I didn't tell the bank I was going to America and I was worried they'd shit themselves and put a stop on the card if I tried taking $200 out at a time. It meant that I was having to go to a cash machine more than once a day, some days.

By now the days were already merging into one, and only looking back at the notes now, to write this, brings some of the memories back. Like this note: 'Pedalled from Butte. Had big shit in Holiday Inn.' Ah, yes. I remember that. At one place, there was a posh campsite, but you needed a code to get in the bog door – perhaps they'd heard rumours about a smelly Englishman camping out in toilets and flicking off the master switch from campsites further up the Great Divide. More often than not I had been shitting at the side of the trail. Once I'd finished, I'd get the thick of it off with a handful of grass, then go in with a biodegradable baby wipe. But faced with the choice of the side of the road or a Holiday Inn, the chain hotel won, pants down.

I parked up outside, left my helmet on the handlebars and walked in with confidence. 'Alright, love,' to the woman behind reception and straight across the lobby like I owned the place.

After that the trail became the hardest going it had been so far. On the way up to the Beaverdam Campground I rode under the busy Interstate 15, which runs all the way from the Mexican border near San Diego, California to the Canadian border in Montana, not far from where I crossed into America. Then I was up and down the Fleecer Ridge, and my Salsa felt a bit out of its depth. Any bike was going to be a compromise over this distance, and descending Mount Fleecer towards Wise River made me wish I was on a downhill mountain bike with decent suspension travel front and rear. On my yellow Salsa, with its rigid back end, I was being battered about and had to keep braking just to stay in control.

Wise River was another memorable stop. A small town that is a big draw for fly-fishing folk, it has two rivers running through it, or near it: Big Hole River and Wise River, with the 9,436-foot Mount Fleecer in the background. I met someone there from Harrogate visiting their relatives. Leaving the town, the trail was dead steep to Elkhorn Hot Springs and then downhill, on past Polaris, before joining the TransAmerica Bicycle Trail for a couple of miles.

I made a note in my pad: 'It's taken two days to get the TT out of my head and I'll only go back if I can ride something different.' I had seen some of the results on the internet when I was in Canada. I didn't want to be in the Isle of Man – I was just being nosey about who was doing what and why. I'd been racing there how many years, without missing one, so it must have been in my head when my mind wandered.

By now, if I'd been following the recommended mileages in the guidebook, I'd be on day 25. Twenty-five days of riding and, except for the Canadian bit, all of it in one US state, Montana. For me, though, it was day six. I'd lost count and the notes in my book were making less sense. I wasn't thinking about England or whatever. I'd turned more robotic. Luckily, the twinge in my Achilles hadn't developed into anything. The only real target I was thinking about was to finish in under 20 days. The record was 14 days, 11 hours and 27 minutes, but I heard later that this was a difficult year because of snow on some of the passes and mud and a fair bit of rain. In 2015, the year before, 26 people did it in under 20 days. In the year I did it, only 16 did, according to the official Trackleaders website.

I think I might have crossed into Idaho, but I didn't even know. For the seventh night I stayed in Warm River

Campground. If I had access to a bog, that's what I'd choose to sleep in. I wanted to be in bed by 11 o'clock, then up at 3.30. I would set my alarm for three and do one snooze, then get up, pack up my stuff, fill up the bladder in my Kriega with water and be on the bike before four. I took my Nokia phone as an alarm. It wouldn't work as a phone out there, but it woke me up, and the battery lasted for 18 days.

On day eight I stopped at a bar on the Togwotee Pass that had a computer in the corner, and I asked if I could use it. I was in the Teton Wilderness, in Wyoming. I got on the internet, sent a few messages back home, saw what progress the top riders in the Tour Divide were making and checked who'd won the Senior TT. It was Michael Dunlop, and he did it setting another outright lap record. Legend. I thought, Shit hot.

I left there and the mud was horrible – mud on top of mud on top of mud. I was off and pushing uphill again.

CHAPTER 12

When I finally stopped pedalling I started to cry

TOGWOTEE PASS WAS a big one – 9,658 feet – and it was followed by the 9,210-foot Union Pass, where the Shoshone National Forest met the Fitzpatrick Wilderness and the Gros Ventre Mountains. Union was brutal, because of the pig-shitty mud and the switchbacks. You could look in the guidebooks and count how many 9,000- and 10,000-foot passes there were on the Tour Divide route, and get it in your head how hard it was going to be, but it wasn't that simple. It wasn't a matter of being at 9,000 feet and knowing the pass was 10,000 feet, and thinking, There's only 1,000 feet of climbing before I'm over the top. No, no. I'd climb to 9,500 feet, then descend to 8,000, then have to climb again to 9,700, then descend to 9,000, then climb to just short of 10,000 feet again, then descend. Bloody hell! Descend and climb, climb, descend – argh! I didn't underestimate the climbing – I knew there was 200,000 feet of climbing in total – but I didn't know what the climbs would be like.

Over Union Pass the mud stuck to everything, I was getting bogged down in the stuff, and it was making the bike weigh even more than it already did. I was wearing cycling shoes that were not made for walking in. Because of their hard plastic soles and metal cleats, you can come a cropper in Caistor Co-op if you turn too quickly to head back down the veg aisle to pick up the taties you forgot – but none of it was bothering me too much. It didn't matter how long the push was up whichever mountain I was on, I knew I'd be at the top before long. The trail would be better, the view would change and I might even have a good downhill run with a pizza or two and a beer at the end of it.

I hadn't expected to feel as good as I did physically. I felt better after a week of hard riding, 19 hours a day with food stops in between, even though I was only sleeping 4 hours a night, on a concrete bog floor, or outdoors on the ground. I thought there'd be a gradual dropping off of energy and power, but it was the opposite. I got fitter through the first week then stayed at that level. I got back to England the fittest I have ever been.

Just after Union Pass I stopped for the night. I didn't know what day it was. I had to look back through my notes in the book to see how many nights I'd slept. It was pissing it down, and I saw a log shed near a farmhouse and decided to shelter in it and get my head together until the rain stopped. I thought the farm dog might come to find me, but I didn't hear a sound. I still wasn't having one single negative thought, and I got my head down for an hour and set off again. According to my guidebook I'd now crossed the Continental Divide nine times since Banff.

From there I was pedalling into a headwind for another 60 miles. It was a slog until the town of Pinedale. I made one note in the guidebook: 'Ready for a stop.' I had a pizza, and the waitress thought I was crackers because I ordered another one for pudding, one of those pizzas that comes folded in half, and a beer.

It was the middle of the day, and I was eating away when the waitress comes towards me with a phone in her hand. She asks, 'Are you Terry?' I thought for a minute and remembered. 'Yeah, I am Terry,' I said. 'Terry Smith.' She said, 'There's a bloke on the phone just checking you're alright.' So, I said, 'Yeah, I'm fine. Who is that?' The waitress asked the caller, who said, 'Stephen.' I didn't know what was going on or who was on the phone. It was only on my mind for half an hour at the most, and then I was back to the job in hand.

When I got home it all became clear. Anyone who was following me on the Trackleaders website could zoom right in on the satellite map and see where I was. My mate Dobby had done that and seen that I'd stopped and there was a café or summat, and worked out that must be where I was. He googled the café's phone number and rang up. But he said his name was Stephen. He's never Stephen, always just Dobby, so I had no idea it was him. Anyway, I couldn't have talked to him, because the rules of the race are you're not supposed to speak to anyone you know while you're on the ride. That is the spirit of the event, and the potential for loneliness is a big part of the mental challenge, but by this stage I loved the feeling of being isolated and relying on my own wits. I had nothing to distract me. No music, no one to talk to except when I stopped for food, nothing but the sound of my tyres on the gravel and mud. And that's how I wanted it.

After the big feed at Pinedale I bought some more food to take with me. I rode 50 miles before stopping, but over half of it was on paved roads, so it wasn't hard going. I was about 40 miles short of Atlantic City, which is neither a city nor anywhere near the Atlantic, when I stopped and slept in the open, at the side of the trail.

The plan was to sleep here and get up early, so I could be in Atlantic City for breakfast time, not arrive there in the middle of the night and have to wait until places opened. Stocking up in Atlantic City was important because the next stretch was 180 miles to a place called Wamsutter, which I think was the longest distance without food. But I missed Atlantic City, because the bloody GPS wasn't clear and these places with big names are sometimes only a few low houses and not much else. Once I realised I'd missed it, I just kept going. I thought I'd be alright, but I ran out of water and was filling up bottles out of ditches and using water-purification tablets to stop me from catching owt. I was hardly carrying any food by this stage of the race, thinking that I'd always be alright to get to the next town for a feed there. This day proved that it wasn't the best idea.

It was a tough, tough day, and I had to ride according to the energy I had. There was a brutal headwind and it was baking. The Great Divide Basin is an area of 3,600 square miles where rivers and creeks don't merge and run to either ocean, but drain into this basin to form temporary lakes before they evaporate. The guidebooks said it was one of the emptiest and driest stretches of the whole ride – just flat, parched-dry nothingness with a few nodding-donkey oil pumps dotted through it. There was nothing to stop the wind, and I was crawling forward at only 7 to 9 mph.

Eventually, I pedalled into Wamsutter, which is just a motorway town, where there was a petrol station. I ate two lots of Subway, pizza, ice cream, crisps, full-fat milk, coffee and Gatorade, and I slept in a ditch behind the Shell garage. It had been the toughest day of the whole trip, but it hadn't broken me.

In October 2014, I'd entered a round of the World Solo 24-hour Mountain Bike Championships at Fort William on the west coast of Scotland. I'd done a few 24-hour races there, and I'd been on the podium with the world champion once before, so I knew what I was getting into. Although I didn't think I was going to come close to winning it, I didn't expect to break down like I did. Partway through the race my head just went. I came in, sat in the footwell of my van and couldn't make any sense of what my mate Tim Coles, my dad or anyone else was trying to say to me. I'd cracked. I did get back on the bike and finish it, but nowhere like as strongly as I expected. Now I think I know why. I'd shared a room with my dad and he was snoring so loudly I couldn't get any sleep. I even ended up leaving the hotel room and trying to sleep in the corridor to escape the noise. And I was light, weighing 67 kilograms. I was 75 kilos going into the Tour Divide. I just don't think I had enough reserves for my body to be able to push on in the Fort William race. So even though I was only getting about four hours' sleep a day after climbing, climbing, climbing all day, and for well over a week, I was ready for it.

I've always been able to sleep nearly anywhere (as long as it's not in a room with my dad), but I took that to extremes on the Tour Divide. After a few hours kipping in the ditch, I headed off towards a six-mile climb to the top of Middlewood Hill.

Somehow I was treating the challenge of it all as much like a robot as I could, and not letting myself get too emotional one way or the other. There were just little bits of high, little bits of low, nothing extreme either way. You have to have the attitude that says, Just get on with it.

I crossed the border into Colorado, a new state at last, and entered the village of Slater. There was a little museum and the owner, a real nice woman, had opened a shop just for Tour Divide riders. I was the first person she'd seen. I bought a load of breakfast bars, bananas and grapes and paid a donation.

Fifteen miles later I was stuck. The route led to a river, but the bridge was down. I waded into the water to see if I could cross, but by the time it was up to my chest and flowing like hell, I knew I couldn't. I found a house to ask someone where I could cross, and they told me that I had to go back another ten miles, then ride another past this, that and the other, and finally get across.

I reckoned the folk behind would know the course better than me and wouldn't have made the same mistake, so I lost a bit of time to them, but, again, I wasn't that bothered. What could I do about it now?

The next decent-sized town was Steamboat Springs, a dead posh place and, by the official mileage, 1,511 miles in. I scribbled a note in the back of the guidebook: 'Started Tuesday 7. Friday 17, Steamboat 1,511 miles. Eleven days, have done 1,511. Only 1,234 to do.' But I'd done more than the official mileage because I'd got lost and had to take official detours. It was about half-seven at night as I pedalled into the outskirts of Steamboat Springs, and all that was going through my mind was, Show me the food. I dived straight into another Subway, giving them a spike in their profits they hadn't expected.

The next morning I got lost again while I was trying to cross the Yampa River. I set off at four in the morning and spent the best part of two hours trying to find the right route. I'd ride to the bottom of this dam, then back up again. The Garmin let me down, because I hadn't downloaded the maps, and it wasn't clear that I had to ride over the top of a dam. I was kicking myself a bit.

By half-six the same morning, Mike Hall, the race leader, caught me. He had taken three days out of me. I quickly saw that he was carrying even less than me.

He was riding a Pivot LES, with 29-inch wheels and Shimano electric gears, all charged off the front hub. It was a light 16 kilograms packed with all his kit, whereas mine was 25 kilos and I'd taken next to nothing. It was his third Tour Divide. He'd done the first in 19 days, and he told me that no one could set a record on their first attempt because there's so much you need to learn. He's a year older than me, and he's from Harrogate, in Yorkshire, but lives in Cardiff.

For the next few hours I rode with Mike, and there was nothing about him that made me think he was superhuman. He was just dead calm and a bit faster than me on the climbs. I knew his packed bike weighed less, but still, he was on it.

We passed through the towns of Radium and Kremmling, not together as in side by side, but in sight of each other. He'd pass me, then I'd pass him when he stopped to change his clothes. I spoke to him a bit, though. I told him that I'd worked out that if we were over halfway and it had taken him three days to catch me, he could pull another three days on me between now and the end. If he was on record pace – 14 days or thereabouts – I'd still finish in 20 days.

I wasn't surprised he'd already taken three days out of me. I'd got lost and I wasn't in the routine, plus I wasn't trying to set a record time, so I'd sit a bit longer having something to eat. It's dead simple: sleep less, ride more.

Well, simple to say, not simple to do. The Tour Divide is not about riding faster, just riding further, every day.

At the end of the day I wrote another note in the book: 'Riding with Mike made me push. I like my own company.' I was riding hard, not hanging about, but Mike made me ride a bit harder than I felt comfortable with at that time. I look back now and part of me thinks I should've tried to stay with him, but it was my first time doing a ride that long so I didn't know what pace I could keep up. It's so important to ride at your own pace in an endurance event like this, and realise that other people might be quicker than you in different parts of the race. You could set off like hell trying to keep up with someone, not knowing that they're going to collapse halfway through and not make the finish.

By the time I reached the Ute Pass I was on my own again. This was another climb that peaked at 10,000 feet. The whole of Colorado is a mile or more above sea level, so these climbs weren't from zero to 10,000 feet, but the air is still thinner when you're at the top.

After the descent there was another stretch of tarmac road, eight miles or so, into Silverthorne. This was another place that seemed dead posh, somewhere I can imagine that people who've made a load of money would buy a holiday home in the mountains. It's not far from Vail, a Colorado ski resort I'd heard of. I like the idea of living in a place like this, but only for a minute.

I know I wouldn't like the reality of it. Still, after not seeing anyone for hours, it was a nice place to roll into as the sun was setting.

There was a good cycle path around Dillon Reservoir, on the other side of Silverthorne. The guidebook reckoned that the reservoir supplied the water for Denver, 50 miles east, through 20 miles of tunnel.

Breckenridge was more of the same, posh as fuck. Between these towns I was passing rare stuff all the time, like a wooden water tank that supplied the old steam locomotives, and riding through areas with names like the Arapaho National Forest. I was never bored.

Ahead of me was the Boreas Pass, at 11,482 feet, one of the highest points of the whole Tour Divide route. I thought it would do me good to sleep up there, giving my body some altitude training while I was resting. It was Saturday night. I'm not big on going out on a Saturday night, never have been, but I've never had a Saturday night quite like this one. It was cold, but not cold enough to keep me awake, and I was out like a light.

I was up and away by 3.30 for a mint section of downhill to Como, then on to Hartsel for an omelette so good I even made a note of it in my book. By the time I walked into the café at eight in the morning, I'd done 40 miles of mainly off-road riding. If I'd been sticking to what the guidebook recommended for a half-keen cyclist's daily average mileages, I'd have just finished day

46, even though the book did say riders could probably manage more. The author had worked out these mileages so no one was stranded from somewhere to get supplies or to a campsite. As it was, I was just beginning day 13.

My first puncture of the trip came on that day too. I hadn't done anything out of the ordinary, just hit a sharp rock in the right, or wrong, place. It was a one-in-a-million chance, but it was going to happen because of the miles I was doing on that terrain. After all, how many million times did those wheels go round? I had tubeless tyres, so I had to take it off the bead and stick a tube in it. In all it took about ten minutes.

In Colorado I was seeing a lot more 4x4s on the remote trails I was riding. Most of the drivers were dead polite and slowed right down. Some didn't and kicked up a load of dust. I can't remember exactly where it was, as a lot of the route is a blur, but I was riding through a tight spot, not much room on either side of the trail and a big drop to one side, in the middle of nowhere, when a load of Jeeps came towards me. They all slowed down and waved. I saw they had all the gear on them, winches on their front bumpers, roll cages, special tow ropes and all that, and it made me wonder, Where are those boys going?

I didn't think any more of it, and got on with the job of pedalling and wondering where my next milkshake was coming from. A couple of hours later I got to the summit of wherever I was, and there was a bloke there, walking on his own. I said, 'Now mate, are you alright?' He explained that he'd had a bit of bother. He'd been out with his mates, all in 4x4s. 'You haven't seen them, have you?' he asked. I told him I had and he said he was at the back, but had got proper stuck and they hadn't noticed and had driven on without him. He was walking to try to get some signal on his phone. He wasn't panicking, though. Then he told me that he knew the route I was taking and I'd go near the campsite they were all staying at. Could I do him a favour and drop a note off? They had a big camp set up, apparently, and I couldn't miss it.

He described where the camp was and wrote a note with his GPS position on a bit of paper ripped out of my notebook. He told me they were the only people on the campsite, so if I pinned the note to one of the tents, his mates could find him from that grid reference. It was two miles out of my way, but no bother.

When I got to their campsite I rooted through all their food and drink, had some milk and biscuits, foraging like Mad Max after the bomb's gone off. I thought I'd been right by him, going out of my way, so it was OK to help myself to a bit of grub. They had loads of food, and I didn't take the piss.

On the trail from Hartsel to Salida I could look out west and see a row of 14,000-foot mountain peaks, called Princeton, Harvard, Yale and Columbia, after the exclusive old universities, and another, Mount Shavano. Bloody impressive.

After a good downhill run I reached Salida, probably the coolest town on the whole route, and home to a mega ice-cream parlour. The whole town was retro – well, not retro, just unchanged since the 1950s. Like Lincolnshire. The next climb was brutal, 12 miles up to the Marshall Pass, where three mountain ranges all met.

After the descent from there I found a café, in Sargents, that was just closing, but the woman who ran it got the grill fired up and made me a load of chicken, bacon, cheese and everything sandwiches, wrapped in tinfoil to take with me. I was just leaving when a northbound cyclist arrived. I'd meet a good few folk riding northbound, starting off in Antelope Wells and heading north. Some were doing it that way for the same reason I set off early, to miss the crowds and do their own thing, but if you're setting off at this time of year you mean business. You're not really just dawdling, so we were on the same wavelength.

He was an English teacher from Texas, who'd lived in England for ages. He asked what I did, and I told him I was a truck mechanic, like I tell everyone. He told me he'd had a few problems with the bike, but he was still doing well.

Then a car pulled up and the bloke driving said, 'Alright, Terry. I know who you are.' He had been following me on the Trackleaders website. It turned out he was a journalist, Neil Beltchenko, who wrote for bikepacker.com, and he was reporting on the race. He just happened to be passing when I was there. Then more bikes turned up.

They all knew about me not really being Terry Smith, but I didn't know how the word had got out and I still don't. They said it had come out of England. I hadn't made a secret about doing the race, so I suppose if someone really wanted to find out they could have looked through the list of entrants. I explained that I was just doing the race for me, and that was why I entered under a pseudonym, but I think I might have still put my hometown as Grimsby, so it wouldn't have taken Poirot to work out who might have been me.

Still, I had a good craic with them, and it was the first time, other than a bit with Mike Hall, that I'd spoken about the Tour Divide with people who really knew what it was. It turns out that Neil was the most hardcore of the lot, and he held the unofficial record. The riders were impressed that I had such well-sorted kit on my first attempt at it. Neil was saying it takes years for some people to get it right.

I packed my sandwiches into the handlebar bag and rode off thinking, That was a bloody great meeting, talking to proper Tour Divide lads. Thirty miles later I slept for a few hours at the side of the trail again and was up at four the next morning. Not far ahead were two 10,000-foot-plus passes, called Cochetopa and Carnero.

South of La Garita I was finding it hard to stay on the trail I was supposed to be on. The out-of-date Garmin and five-year-old guidebook were limiting me a bit, but I was alright. To retell it now it could sound monotonous: pedalling, Subway sandwiches, more pedalling, getting up at 3.30 or 4, pedalling, another 10- or 11,000-foot pass to climb … the truth is, I was loving it. My arse was hurting a bit, but I was tilting my seat one notch down, then one notch up, every couple of days to take the pressure off different parts of my backside. I was sleeping naked at night, when it wasn't too cold, and blathering on nappy-rash cream, because it's a bit antiseptic. My arse was red raw in places, and I didn't want to get an infection. Every morning I had to climb back into the clammy, damp *Sideburn* magazine T-shirt I wore for the whole trip.

I was 20-odd miles short of New Mexico, the last state line I would cross, when I stopped for the night at Stunner Campground, north of Platoro. It was a dead nice campsite, with a cabin you could sleep in and a shed full of logs for the fire. All you had to do was get a key off the ranger, but I arrived too late and everything was deserted. I knew that if I rode on to Platoro I'd be too late for food, so I gently jimmied the lock on the campsite bogs and slept in there. They were the best bogs of the trip – there was even a candle so I had a bit of heat. It was spot on. Other than sleeping in the old-fashioned covered wagon, in Ovando, I'd slept rough every night since leaving Banff. And the wagon was the type you see in cowboy films, so it was still fairly rough.

There was a stream to fill up my bottles with in the campsite and I left at 4.30. Just near Horca, 30 miles into the day's ride, I saw a sign on a shop saying 'Open at 8'. It was quarter to, so I went off for a shit in the woods and, dead on eight, I knocked on the door. A woman answered, 'Howdy.'

'Oh, I'm dead sorry,' I said, 'but can I just buy some stuff?'

'Yeah, no problem. We're just having a cup of coffee.' I sat and had a cup of coffee with the family and their dogs. Again, they were the nicest folk. I told them what I was doing, bought a load of cake and set off again, feeling the fittest I had ever been.

By now I only had about 700 miles to go and was confident that this ride was not going to break me. Other than my backside, I was in good shape, and mentally I felt the strongest ever, with not one crack.

Less than 20 miles after my breakfast stop, I rode into New Mexico, the last US state I had to cycle through.

A proper find, the kind of place that helped make the Tour Divide so special, was the Shack in the tiny village of Cañon Plaza. A brother and sister had opened a shack to feed riders doing the Tour Divide, but it was the mother who was keeping an eye on the tracking website today and knew that someone called Terry Smith was close by. I was 85 miles from where I'd had coffee and cake with the family and their dogs, so I was ready for food, and there wasn't really anywhere else to eat from there to Cuba, New Mexico, 120 miles away. I had three Pot Noodles, tuna, biscuits, crisps, Gatorade – just chucking anything within reach into my gob.

I was still stuffed four miles later when I rode through Vallecitos, also known as Dog Alley, because it's where the stray dogs go mad chasing riders. I thought they were going to rip my calf muscles off, they were going so mental.

I slept in a farmyard near El Rito and was up again at four and into another hard day of climbing. On the far side of Abiquiú I could see Cerro Pedernal, a mesa, the kind of flat-topped mountain with steep sides you see in cowboy films or adverts for Marlboro cigarettes. I picked up another two punctures, which, along with the amount of climbing, meant that it took eight hours to ride from Abiquiú (pronounced Ab-uh-queue) to Cuba, even though it was only about 80 miles. The book recommended covering the distance between the two towns in two days, with the first day being only 23 miles of riding. It said: 'Today's mileage may appear short, but the effort expended to make those 23.2 miles will be considerable.' I'd been riding before the eight hours for this stretch, and I was still riding long after.

I bought some extra inner tubes in Cuba, because I was out of spares and the slits in my tubes were so big I couldn't repair them. The new tubes weren't the right size, so I hoped I wouldn't have to use them, because it would be a struggle. Luckily, I didn't get another flat.

The scenery was half-desert, half-forest, and dry with no mud – or no mud when I was going through, anyway. When it's wet it's supposed to be horrible. The scenery was not quite as beautiful as Montana, but still nice – mountains and low trees nearly as far as the eye could see.

In Cuba, I was weighing up what to do and where to stay. This was the biggest part of the strategy for the Tour Divide, knowing when to stop so you're passing places that sell food and drink when they're open. It never entered my head that I'd have to plan like that before I started the ride, but I learned pretty quickly.

The tailwind out of Cuba was mega. I'd had days with bad headwind, and it had been a real slog, but this was the other side of the coin and I was doing 30 mph for about three hours, making hay while the sun shone. If it's good, just keep going.

The wind started to turn at about 11 at night, the time I usually packed in riding for the day, so it made sense to stop. My lights were run off a dynamo in the hub, a dead clever thing, but as soon as I stopped pedalling it was pitch black. I took my head torch off the handlebars, and clicked it on to have a look around as I decided where I was going to camp for the night. It was all sandy with plenty of cacti, so I found a fairly clear patch, kicked some rocks out of the way and thought to myself, This will have to do. As soon as I turned off my torch a light came on, shining right at me, and a man's voice asked what I was doing. I thought, Fuck! What's this? I told the voice I was just having forty winks. Then he said, 'You don't want to sleep here,' and then I'm sure he added, 'There's a Bigfoot about.'

He said, 'There's a house over the road and we saw you looking out here. Come and kip in our garden shed.' They were a Native American family, Indians as they used to be called – a lad, his mum and dad – and they were more lovely people that I met on the ride. They brought me a cup of coffee and an apple. They hadn't heard of the Tour Divide, so I sat with the son, who'd have been 20 or so, and showed him the guidebook.

I asked him what town I was near, and he explained that we were on the reservation. I'm not sure if they were Apaches or Navajos or what. They didn't have a clue who I was, so they weren't being nice to me because I'd been on the telly. They were just nice people. I loved being anonymous on tour in the middle of a massive foreign country.

I left their shed at four in the morning and I was in Grants, where the Tour Divide trail crossed Interstate 40, which is part of the old Route 66, at eight. There was a big truck stop so I treated myself to my first shower since leaving the hotel in Banff. I was about 2,400 miles in and on my seventeenth day of riding, so I didn't know if I needed a shower or not, but I was going to have one anyway and it was mega. It cost me $11, though. I thought it was dear, but they gave me soap and the use of a towel. You had to book your shower, so while I was waiting I went in the diner and ordered summat called Chester's chicken. I was tucking into it when someone came to find me and told me my shower was ready. I took my chicken with me and sat naked on a bench in the shower, eating it. I caught the reflection of myself in a mirror and couldn't believe how much weight I'd lost. I was sat there, filling my face and thinking, Who's that? I looked like I'd escaped from a prisoner-of-war camp. If I hadn't have been biking I'd have been a fat bugger, the amount of rubbish I was eating.

I had been thinking about the infections I was risking and was keen to wash my backside and feet. I didn't want anything like an infected sore to stop me, because I wasn't having any problems with fitness or motivation. I finished my fried chicken, stepped under the shower and watched as the water ran brown with dust, flies and 16 days of whatever else. I could hardly believe what was coming out of my hair, and it had been cut short with clippers just before I left Canada.

I washed my cycling shorts and socks in the sink, but I didn't wash my T-shirt and I don't know why. Perhaps I subconsciously wanted to experiment with how it would smell after being worn for 20 days of nearly 3,000 miles of cycling. The answer wasn't unexpected: ripe.

Back on the bike, this time on Route 66 for a while then on a trail to Pie Town. And that was a slog. After 130-odd miles I rolled into Pie Town, arriving just before the shops closed. What a place. There was a pie shop, of course, but not selling meat pies, only fruit pies. They're missing a trick. I ate two apple pies when I was there – family sized, not Mr Kipling's – and took a cherry one with me. I also had a cheeseburger and a quesadilla.

Also in Pie Town is the Toaster House, a hostel for riders and hikers doing the Tour Divide or the TransAmerica Trail. You can't miss it, with its knackered toasters fixed to the fence all around it and loads of old shoes nailed to the outside wall. Inside, there are maps pinned up and a load of stuff in the fridge. This hostel was operated on an honesty-box system, so you paid for what you took. There were beds and seats – it was brilliant. I wasn't the only one staying there that night. There was a hiker, heading northbound, who I had met in the pie shop. He walked bits of the Continental Divide every year. He asked if I was staying there, and that sort of made my mind up that I would. It was six in the afternoon by the time I'd finished filling my face, so my plan was to get going at midnight and have a right good push through the Gila Wilderness, a section that's described as the most brutal, because of the heat. It's a desert. It's not like the Sahara, because there are loads of trees, but it's as dry as a bone. People I spoke to said, 'Have you been through the Gila yet?' They pronounced it 'Hee-la', and it made me think it would heal me, like they say in Lincolnshire when something you're about to do is dead hard. 'That'll heal ya.' It's like bad meaning good. Even Mike Hall had said, 'Are you ready for the Gila, mate?' And that was, what, a week ago? Setting off when I planned to meant that I'd be doing the lion's share of it in the cool of the night.

I wanted to get the brunt of the climbing done before four or five in the afternoon, when the heat was worst. People talk about the midday sun, but I always thought the late afternoon felt the hottest. The bloke who was staying in the Toaster House told me where I could scoop up water, but it needed purifying.

I gave my bike a check over, had a yarn with the hiker for an hour and set the alarm on my phone for 11 before getting my head down. I hadn't had any bother sleeping since leaving the hotel in Banff, but I couldn't settle on this night because I knew I had such a big day ahead of me. The climbs weren't mental – 9,000 feet or thereabouts – and Pie Town is nearly one-and-a-half miles above sea level, so, again, I wouldn't be climbing from the sea-level base of a mountain to the top, but it was the continuous slog of hairpin after hairpin, at an altitude I wasn't used to before I left England. I work in Grimsby. You can't get more sea level than that unless you grow gills.

I woke up at ten, ahead of the alarm, and forced myself back to sleep for the extra hour, then I woke up again by myself, checked my watch and it was three in the morning. I'd set my alarm for eleven in the morning by mistake. It was a bit of a bastard, but you can't let these things knock you off course. I was already thinking, Oh, it's alright. I had some porridge at the Toaster House, got my gear on and set off.

My plan was out of the window, but you have to stay positive. It's the negative thoughts that will stop someone from finishing a ride like this. The negative thoughts; the broken bones; being attacked by a grizzly bear; having your calf muscle chewed off by a stray dog; riding off the side of a cliff; sunstroke; dehydration; hypothermia ... but mainly the negative thoughts.

Then, three hours in, my gears stopped working. I'd done a load of research about what gears to run and decided on a Rohloff Speedhub. It's different to any of the gear systems I have on my other bikes. Most mountain bikes have front and rear derailleurs, with a mechanism moving the chain from sprocket to sprocket.

The Rohloff hub I had fitted has all the gears within the rear hub, like an old-fashioned Sturmey-Archer set-up. And the Rohloff has 14 gears. I liked the idea of it being enclosed so it wouldn't get damaged by rocks or worn by all the dust and grit and shit. In the end it wasn't the hub that had stopped working, but the controls to change gear. I squatted at the side of the trail, with the few essential tools I had with me, trying to fix it, but it wasn't having it, so I had to single-speed it. By that I mean I had to choose one gear that would let me climb, but wasn't so low that it was useless on the flatter sections where I'd have to pedal like hell to get anywhere. I knew that some lads did the whole Tour Divide route single-speed, and in very quick times, so I was still staying positive. I set off again.

The landscape was rockier with nowhere near as many trees now, but I was making good time, averaging 15 mph, until the climbing started. The temperature was rising into the early 40s, which meant I had to push it up some of the climbs.

This was where I felt I needed the most mental strength of the whole ride. Although the route is designed to follow the Continental Divide, and is never more than 50 miles from it, the Continental Divide is like the equator – it's geographical, not manmade, and the trail can't follow it exactly for long. But for eight miles that day, I was on the line of the Continental Divide itself.

I was having more bother with the gears when a fit bird in a 4x4 pulled up next to me. 'Are you alright?' she said. I told her I was, and I asked where Pinos Altos was. I knew that was the peak of the climbing and the highest point of the rest of the route. I thought, or hoped, it would be about two miles, but she said, 'Ten miles, maybe more.' It was nine at night, the light had just gone, and I thought, Oh, fuck.

She said, 'Just chuck your bike in the back, no bother.' But I wasn't even tempted. Earlier in the day, when I was pushing up the mountain on tiptoes because it was so steep, I was thinking, If some bugger comes past now I'm getting a lift. But as soon as someone handed it on a plate, I thought, Nah, you're alright, love. There was no way I was getting to within a day of the end and caving in, however hard it got. No way.

By the time I got to Silver City at just gone 11, I was starving. I hadn't eaten properly since Pie Town, and there are 185 miles of desert and mountains between those two towns. All I had set off with was one pie in my bag. I found a 24-hour McDonald's and started filling my face: chocolate milkshakes, two of them, apple pies, burgers. I was back and forth to the counter, ordering more every time I finished what was in front of me, and no one gave me a second look. It's America, it must be what they do. I finally finished filling my face at one in the morning. I didn't get sick of eating on this trip, because it had to be done. There wasn't much else happening apart from pedalling, so I would look forward to eating, and eating till I could eat no more was alright. I don't think I could face another Subway now, though.

I knew there was only 150 miles to Antelope Wells and the end, and that there was not much climbing left. When I'd been planning the ride, back in England, I thought I'd push to the end from Silver City, without stopping. Now I was here, and because I'd had such a hard time getting up to Pinos Altos, riding single-speed, I decided I'd have a few hours' sleep.

I slept in the back of McDonald's car park without a care in the world. I've seen rats as big as Jack Russells around the bins in McDonald's car parks in Britain, all of them enjoying the cold and greasy all-you-can-eat rodent buffet, but there could have been a herd of them filling their furry faces inches from my head and I wouldn't have noticed. Seventeen nights spent sleeping in different degrees of rough had toughened me up, no doubt about it.

My temporary home for the night, and I mean Silver City, not the McDonald's car park, got its name from nearby mines for the precious metal. The town's claim to fame is being the childhood home of Billy the Kid, the outlaw, gunfighter and murderer. It was the first place he was jailed and the first place he escaped from jail.

I got up at four and walked back into the McDonald's

for more food. While I was waiting, a fella with his mate got talking, worked out I was British and said, 'You heard about Brexit?' This was the early hours of Saturday morning, so we were already out, but I explained that I didn't know anything about it. I filled my face again: three pancakes, sausage, apple pie, Egg McMuffin, two coffees, and took more for the journey as I set off for the finish in Antelope Wells.

The first 18 miles were on tarmac, State Highway 90, and easy going. At the end of that stretch there was a cool shop where the route turned off to follow a dirt trail again. I stopped for two ice creams and more coffee, sticking to the rule of eating and drinking when I got the chance. I had started thinking I had finished. I was still 100 miles away, but I knew I'd done it, though there was still a sting in the tail.

The countryside was more or less flat, but as hot as an oven. I was into the Chihuahuan Desert, which stretches into both America and Mexico. For some reason, with about 20 miles to go, I started having my first negative thoughts of the whole ride, wondering if I could keep going. But I didn't let them bother me for too long – I just kept spinning the pedals. There was a really bad headwind that wasn't helping. After hundreds of miles of rough trails my fingers went numb from the vibration, and months later I was still struggling with grip.

The miles clicked down, like they had for the past 18

days, and then I saw it: Antelope Wells, and the Mexican border with its long fence. There aren't any antelopes or wells there and, according to the internet, it's the least-used border crossing of the 43 that dot the 1,989-mile border between the two countries. It's remote, alright. There were some guards at the post, and that was it. They didn't bother coming out of their border post. And there's nothing to say you've survived the Tour Divide. No banner to ride under or someone with a flag. Nothing, exactly like Banff. If you're doing a ride like this it's enough to know yourself that you've finished and you did it.

Sharon was there to meet me. I hadn't spoken to her since I left Heathrow, three weeks ago, and she'd had to organise a load of stuff to get there, flying into Phoenix, Arizona, getting a rental car and finding Antelope Wells. I already had a plan B if she wasn't there to meet me, but she was. She'd been there, in the baking heat, for six hours with a Subway sandwich waiting for me. I was impressed. Plan B, if she hadn't been there, was getting back on the bike to Deming, 80-odd miles away, where I would hopefully get on a bus or something to Phoenix airport.

When I finally stopped pedalling I started to cry. I've never done a race that's made me cry. I don't know if it was the relief of doing what I set out to do or what. It was the strangest feeling. No snivelling or shoulders shaking or anything, just water coming out of my face. Where the heck was that coming from?

I had a beard, for the first time ever, because I hadn't shaved for three weeks. I was a bit sunburnt, but not too bad. Sharon took a couple of photos of me by the Antelope Wells sign. Another woman was waiting for her fella, who was a couple of hours behind me, so we had her take a photo of me and Sharon together. There wasn't any big celebration. It just ended. One minute I was cycling across America, the next I wasn't.

I had cycled 2,745 miles, and probably a bit more, in 18 days and 6 hours, quicker than the time that established the Tour Divide record, set by Matthew Lee in 2008, of 19 days and 12 hours. I averaged 149 miles per day, every day. I'd soon learn that Mike Hall, the Yorkshireman living in Cardiff who I met on the route, set a new record of 13 days, 22 hours and 51 minutes. Impressive.

I took the wheels off the bike and stuck it in the back of the rental car, and I climbed in the passenger seat. Sharon never complains if I haven't had a wash for a while, but she said I stunk the car out that day.

We headed towards Phoenix and stopped in a cheap motel, where I had my second shower of the trip. Sharon brought my trainers, shorts, kecks and clean T-shirts, so I could finally get out of the clothes I'd been wearing for going on three weeks.

Even though I'd been sleeping rough and eating shit, I wasn't bothered about finding a luxury hotel or treating myself. We just went to a trucker's caff, like a Little

Chef, which was attached to the motel. I think Sharon wouldn't have minded a few days' holiday in America, but I was ready to get home. I sent Spellman an email to see if he could sort us an earlier flight. He got on the case and arranged one for the next day. I was in bed for nine and slept till eight the next morning. Nothing radical.

I wasn't sure before if the whole Tour Divide experience was going to break me, but it hadn't. It made me realise that if I put my mind to it I can do anything. Instead of wondering how, or even if, it had changed me, I had the same feeling as I did driving home after the wall of death. Both these things had taken so much time and effort to build up to. With the wall of death it was building the bike, learning how to ride the wall, then going as fast as humanly possible on it live on TV. For the Tour Divide it was riding further and for longer than I ever had, relying on myself and sleeping rough. At the end of both of them I wasn't looking forward to relaxing and taking it easy – I was itching for the next big challenge. I just wasn't sure what it should be.

CHAPTER 13

Racing hasn't retired me, I've retired from racing

BEFORE LEAVING FOR the Tour Divide I told Andy Spellman and North One that I wasn't making decisions about any future TV work until I got back. If I wasn't halfway through filming a programme, like I was with some of the *Speed* series, everything was put off, because

I didn't know if it was going to change my attitude towards the job. The telly stuff I do seems to go down well and folk want me to make more of it, but I still turn a lot down. I do enjoy making the programmes now. I never watch them – I doubt many people who are on telly watch themselves, but perhaps they do. I'd love it if I could just make the programmes and they were never shown, because I enjoy the process, the people I work with and the folk I meet in the course of it all. The main thing I have a bit of a problem with is the attention it brings, but living where I do and how I do, not going out much and not living in a big city, it isn't too bad. I came back from America thinking that I've got the balance about right. Trucks, telly, motorbikes, biking, doing a few barrow jobs for mates, when they need help, like skimming a car cylinder head or porting bike cylinder heads. One thing it really made me realise was that I should have given up racing motorbikes earlier than I did. I'm writing this a few days after getting back, and I'm not sure how much the experience has changed me, but that was the big thing, the light bulb going on.

Riding the Tour Divide couldn't have been further away from the Isle of Man TT, both physically and mentally. It reminded me that most people are genuinely nice, when I was beginning to think that a lot of them were rude. I was getting the feeling that people had seen me on telly and only wanted to talk to me to tell someone else that they'd talked to me, and not because they were into what I was into or they had something interesting to say. America made me realise that it's not all like that. The people I met on the Tour Divide didn't know I'd been on telly a few times – they just wanted to help the person they'd just met, even though I smelt like a dead badger. They'd open their shop early, invite me in for a hot drink or fire the grill back up, even though they were just heading home, because they're nice people and they want to help other people. I've got manners and I ask for things politely – I think I'm a nice person, and I like it when other people are.

I worked out that, as an amateur racer, which is what I've always been, I can't do better than I've already done. To do it properly would mean me returning from the Tour Divide, racing in all the remaining 2016 British Superbike rounds, then doing all the rounds at the beginning of next year, to give me the best start into the TT. But I can accept that I haven't won a TT, because I didn't dedicate my whole existence to it. In the same way, I know that if I want to set a record at the Tour Divide I have to dedicate my life to it, and I don't want to do that. There's other stuff I want to do, and I'm happy knowing that I won't set the Tour Divide record or win a TT.

The only way I'll go back to the TT is if they let me race something oddball. They allowed Bruce Anstey to race Padgett's Honda RCV213V-S in 2016, they let the Norton and the Suter 500 two-stroke race as well, all oddball stuff that, I think, makes the race more interesting. If they'll let me ride something I build in my shed I'll go back and try to get in the top 20, but if they don't I'm not bothered.

The 2016 TT was a bad year for deaths, but that didn't make any difference one way or the other to the way I thought about it. I knew Paul Shoesmith a bit. They reckon his front tyre blew out on Sulby Straight, one of the fastest sections of the track. There's not a lot you can do to avoid that happening, and there's nothing you can do to save it if it happens to you.

Another racer I really liked, Billy Redmayne, died after crashing at Scarborough in the 2016 Spring Cup National. I'd met Billy and his mates at Wanganui, the last time I was out in New Zealand, and we'd talked about all sorts of daft conspiracy theories. He was a nice bloke. These deaths don't affect my choice to continue on the roads, and they're going to happen, now and then, whether I'm racing or not, but it's one more thing in the negative column. If I'm not enjoying it, and people are dying, then you really do have to ask yourself, Why am I doing this?

John McGuinness was quoted on the internet as saying he'd rather stick live wasps up his arse than ride 2,745 miles on a pushbike. He said, 'I just can't get why anyone would want to do a bicycle race instead of the

TT.' He also reckoned I was getting money for the Tour Divide, which, you'll know by now, is wrong. It ended up costing me thousands and not earning me anything, and I knew that before I set off. I work hard. I like going to Moody's on a Saturday morning and thinking, I'm on time-and-a-half here, and I like buying stuff, CNC machines, daft cars, new pushbike bits, but I'm not motivated by money. I'm motivated by job satisfaction. I don't do stuff that I don't want to do, no matter how much it's going to pay. And the Tour Divide was nothing about money at all. It never was.

My dare to the lads at the sharp end of the TT would be: You do what I've done, not necessarily a mountain-bike race, but something that would push you in another way, and then come back and tell me I'm mad for missing the TT. They're operating on autopilot. Every year is the same, the build-up with the North West 200, the TT, then the same run down to the Ulster. At the NEC show they start talking about what they're going to do next season, then the build-up again beginning in the spring with all the testing in Spain and Ireland, tyre testing at Castle Combe. And they say I'm mad for missing the TT? If they did what I've done they might realise there is more to life. As good as the TT was, and what an event, why was I doing it? Why? My dad raced bikes, so I raced bikes. I loved it and it opened a load of doors. I got alright at road racing so the natural thing was to race the TT. Then that's it, you're in and the blinkers are on. The only time you get out of that vicious circle is if you get shit and no one wants you any more. Then what do you do? What Steve Parrish, James Whitham and Neil Hodgson do, which is talk about it. Racing hasn't retired me, I've retired from racing. Perhaps they're all trying to avoid getting a real job, and if that's what they want, great. But I love my job, and I was looking forward to coming back to work on the trucks. I got on the earliest flight I could from Arizona so I could get back to it.

So, I've had it with motorbike racing. I've realised that I maybe should have stopped three years earlier. It was only not racing at all in 2016 that made me realise I wasn't enjoying it and I didn't miss it.

As soon as I got back from the Tour Divide the Tyco TAS BMW team were already asking if I wanted a ride at Kirkistown. Lovely lads, who I really like spending time with, but what's the point in riding a bike I know at Kirkistown, somewhere I've done hundreds of laps around? What am I going to learn? Sod all.

Another thing I thought was that I'd never want to see a pushbike again, but by the end of the Tour Divide I was thinking, I've got all this fitness, I don't want to waste it. So I got home and tried to enter the Salzkammergut Trophy, a mountain-bike race in Austria, but the entries had closed. It was just as well because I need to concentrate on getting my turbo bike ready instead.

I won't ride the Tour Divide bike again. I retired it and it's sat in Louth Cycle Centre. I bought almost all the bits for the bike, £2,400 worth – hubs, bags, charging gear – and Hope gave me brakes and crankset. I might take some bits out of it and build another bike. If I was going to do something like the Tour Divide again I'd start with a proper mountain bike. There was a lot more mountain biking than I'd thought there'd be, and it would be lighter than the Salsa.

A few days after getting back from America I was in at work, and Belty was snorting up phlegm, making a horrible noise that was getting right on my nerves. I asked him to stop, but he kept doing it. Then I warned him not to do it, but he kept at it. The next thing I know, I've got him by the throat. I couldn't understand why at first. All I can think is that being on my own, with no one asking me anything, no one relying on me and no one to deal with, gave me a very short fuse. And that short fuse was there when I had to go back and deal with people. Maybe I need another big ride.

I want to cycle to Magadan, on the far side of Russia. That would be something to aim for, wouldn't it?

CHAPTER 14

Gina and Nicky's netball lasses and free butties from the wagon

THE MAJESTIC ROCKIES, the Teton mountain range, the Gila Wilderness, the Chihuahuan Desert ... the contrasts in the scenery I saw on the Tour Divide were amazing. Not Radio 1 'amazing', but properly amazing. I rode on fire roads through woods and forests, concentrating on not getting my eye poked out by a low branch, then there would be a clearing in the trees, and in the distance I could see snow-capped mountains. I'd look down at my Garmin and realise, This is taking me dead south, those mountains are south: I'm going over them. I wasn't worried or apprehensive, it was just a case of, Right, I'm going over those buggers. Very matter of fact.

After the Tour Divide, I flew back with Sharon and we landed at Heathrow. I cycled into work the next day to prove to myself that I could get back on the bike straight after all that. Then I had a few days off the bike to let my body recover. The following Monday, I'd been back just short of a week and it was a beautiful morning. I shouldn't really have biked to work, because I was still a bit sore, but I couldn't resist it. I was a good two-thirds of the way there, just over Riby Top, and riding down Riby Drag, so called because it's a bit of a struggle for a truck to get up it. I looked up and out and saw the view of Grimsby, Immingham Dock, the Humber Estuary and Spurn Point on the Yorkshire side of the Humber, all spread out in front of me under the morning sun. I reckoned it was as beautiful as anything I'd seen in America.

My mate Benny and his family emigrated to New Zealand – I visited them a couple of times when I raced at Wanganui over Christmas – but they moved back to Lincolnshire while I was on the Tour Divide. Benny explained that he couldn't have the same standard of living over there as he could here without doing daft amounts of overtime at work. They'd been out there just short of three years when they moved back. Benny and his wife, Jaquina, are happy to be back. He returned to a job earning more than he did when he left, and he says nowt's changed, but he likes that. I like that about the place too.

When Sacha Baron Cohen's comedy *Grimsby* was being filmed, a local politician came round to Moody's to have a word with us. He was worried that it was going to portray Grimsby in a negative way. I described the visit in *When You Dead, You Dead*, but that was before I, or anyone, had seen the film.

I was on a two-day filming job down in Bedford, getting the hang of the pedal-powered hot-air balloon I'm hoping to fly over the English Channel (that's not a sentence you write every day), when *Grimsby* was released. Unusually for me, I didn't drive home to try to get something done in the shed between the two days of filming, then have to drive back to the TV location at stupid o'clock the next morning. Instead, I stayed in a hotel with the North One lot, and someone had the idea of going to the pictures to see *Grimsby*.

I like Sacha Baron Cohen's characters. Borat is a big favourite, and even though I think it was filmed in

Essex, I reckon he got *Grimsby* spot on. His accent is pure Grimsby, just like Moody's. The film, and the actor, have been criticised for the way the working classes are portrayed, but it's a comedy – it's supposed to be a funny caricature, not a documentary. I reckon only those who recognise some of themselves in it – and wish they didn't – would be offended by it.

Sacha Baron Cohen plays Nobby, a waster and football hooligan who deep down is a good bloke. He hasn't seen his brother for years, and when they meet he finds out that his brother is a top secret agent. I don't know if I was just in the mood for summat daft, but I found it funny, especially the elephant orgy.

I was born in Grimsby and work in Grimsby, but I've never lived in the town that is home to about 90,000 people. I'm happy to be associated with it, though. I can call it a shithole, because I grew up around there, but you can't if you don't live there. It's my shithole. There are nice bits and rough bits, like everywhere. The rough bits are in the top three most deprived areas in the country, according to government reports from a few years back. But Grimsby, or Great Grimsby, to give the place its proper name, has everything I need. It's a handy place for me, and I'm never stuck for much. There's always someone around who can help you out of a fix. There are 500 food-related companies in the area. When I looked into it I read that there are more pizzas made in Grimsby than anywhere else in Europe.

All those food companies are supplied and served by thousands of trucks, which is why there's such a strong haulage industry, with all the suppliers and specialists that support the road haulage game in the area.

The downsides of Grimsby? I can't think of any. I don't think the people are any different in Grimsby – you get arseholes wherever you go. I just try to steer clear of them. I'm not worried about there not being a lot of culture. I'm not much of a night-out man. I like going to see live bands when one takes my fancy, but I don't mind travelling to see them and, anyway, the Picturebooks came to Grimsby and played Yardbirds, the local biker bar. They were brilliant.

When I decided I was going to write another book, I wanted the cover to be something a bit gritty. I went exploring down by the fish docks for somewhere that could be an interesting backdrop. Fifty or sixty years ago, Grimsby was said to be home to the biggest fishing fleet in the world, but, because of the Cod Wars with Iceland, there are hardly any trawlers fishing out of Grimsby any more. The dock area I found was like a self-contained, run-down, half-deserted town, overlooked by the 300-foot-tall Dock Tower that was built in 1852. It's a dead clever relic of the Industrial Revolution that could hold 30,000 gallons of water which was pumped into it. The pressure of the water, sat at 200 feet above the ground, was then used to provide hydraulic power for the machinery on the docks.

The name of the town comes from the Norse for Fisherman's Village, and Danish Vikings settled here in AD 9. Most of the fish are from Iceland, but some are still processed in works down on Grimsby, whether it's filleting or smoking. The docks are fascinating, like the land that time forgot. You could film a zombie apocalypse film down there and not have to change a thing or even tell anyone. You'd just have to stop the odd truck or Transit van until you'd finished your shot. And you'd only know about the place if you lived round here. I don't know what will happen to it. Parts of it are falling to bits. If it was in London it would have all been converted to fancy flats, but it's Grimsby, and no one wants to live by the docks or invest in doing them up.

When I was on the Tour Divide I found a cycle shop in Whitefish, Montana, where I stopped to buy some new pedals after one of mine had broke. The couple who owned it had been touring about on bicycles, looking for a new place to live, when they rode into Whitefish and decided, This is the place, and stayed. That was back in 1980. No place I've visited has ever grabbed me like that. I've been to a few countries around the world, and there's nowhere that I'd rather be than round here. Only New Zealand has come close, and it's still not here.

I like that I can do deals with the local folk. Take Gina

and Nicky, who run the butty van near work. They're rum as hell, but I like them. A few years ago they said, 'Come and hand out the trophies for the end-of-season Grimsby and District Senior Netball League awards, and we'll give you free butties for the year.' You'd do the same, wouldn't you? When *Top Gear* come knocking, 'Sorry, I'm busy,' but Gina and Nicky's netball lasses and free butties from the wagon? I'm there!

I've got a good mixture of stuff round here, racing pushbikes, building motorbikes and cars, work, a good few routes to cycle home, friends I've known for years, family, a decent house and mates with local farms where I can ride my dirt tracker. I like it so much that I haven't bought a summer getaway in Monaco or Spain. I've bought one on the beach south of Cleethorpes.

I keep wondering, What's the next thing? But it's not through wanting to escape Lincolnshire – it's all about the challenge. And once it's over I always think, I can't wait to get back.

CHAPTER 15

I could show them a front wheel and they knew what was coming

BECAUSE I AVOIDED being eaten by a Montana grizzly, it meant I could race at my favourite motorcycle event of the year. By the middle of July 2016 it had been over 11 months since I'd crashed at the Ulster, and I realised

I was looking forward to a motorbike race for the first time in years. I'm not saying I hadn't enjoyed racing motorcycles for years – I loved racing, but I'd been going from one meeting to the next to the next with my head up my arse. I wasn't really looking forward to them, not even the Southern 100, which I loved once I was there, because I was flat out to get done at work and then rush to the boat.

The run-up to the 2016 Dirt Quake was different. I was just going from there to there to there, and I found myself thinking, Oh, a bit of racing. That'll be alright. And on something stupid an' all.

Dirt Quake was the idea of *Sideburn* magazine. Before Dirt Quake, there was an event called Rollerburn, held at Newark Showground at the end of 2011. It was also organised by *Sideburn*, the coolest motorbike magazine ever. Rollerburn was a mixture of a motorbike custom show, an art show and a roller derby match, with bands playing at one end of the hall and a skateboard ramp in the middle. The whole roller derby thing was mega, and at the end of the night I took part in an indoor drag race against Gary Inman, the editor of *Sideburn*, and Charlie Chuck, the mad-haired comedian who was Uncle Peter in Vic Reeves and Bob Mortimer's *The Smell of Reeves and Mortimer* TV show in the mid-nineties.

We raced down the middle of the exhibition hall on matching dirt-track race bikes, each of us towing a roller-derby lass on her rollerskates. It was like the 1975 film *Rollerball*. We were even wearing helmets painted to exactly match the teams from the film. Charlie Chuck was only taught how to ride a bike a week before the Rollerburn show, just so he could take part in this race. Next thing, he's lining up between me and Gary, and we've all got tattooed lasses from the Lincolnshire Bombers Roller Girls team in short shorts, fishnets and long socks, crouching down and hanging on to special handles on the back of three Co-Built Rotax race bikes.

The race was supposed to be a bit of fun and a spectacle, and it was, but Gary got off the line quicker than me, and I wasn't having that, so I gave the 600 cc dirt tracker a bit of a handful and overtook him, with Charlie Chuck not that far behind, cackling like a madman. He was mental, and now that I think back, he wasn't even wearing a helmet. Unsurprisingly, I hadn't practised racing with a roller-girl on the back, so I think I went a bit quick for the lass. Her racing name was Catfight Candy, and she got into a bit of a speed wobble over 45 mph, fell and ended up with a bit of friction burn from the polished concrete floor. Some of those roller-derby women are as hard as nails, and she was still smiling, happy that we'd won.

Rollerburn was a proper good do. It's where I first met Paul from Krazy Horse. They had a display of bikes and their Airstream caravan, and it was the first time I met the Racefit lot too, who would end up making the exhaust

It's a 15-mile climb to get to the top of Marshall Pass. Hard going.

An ice cream in Salida, Colorado, and my titanium spork with something healthy to eat, for a change.

I crossed Route 66 the day after I slept on the Indian reservation.

A pie in Pie Town, New Mexico.

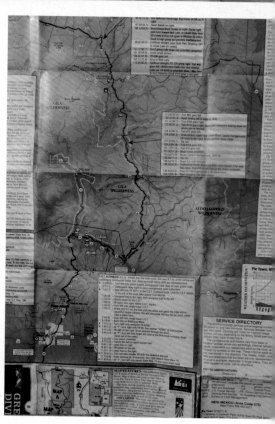

I'll have everything on the blackboard, please.

The Toaster House, the hostel where I spent the night in Pie Town.

The map on the wall of the Toaster House. By now I knew my GPS map was out of date, so I took this photo in case I needed to zoom in and refer to it. You can see the Gila Wilderness, which lay ahead of me.

At the end of the Tour Divide, looking a bit the worse for wear.

Nigel the dog trying on a
Nigel the dog hat.

Dave, one of the Foxes' ducks
that Nigel got a grip on.

That's not my van.

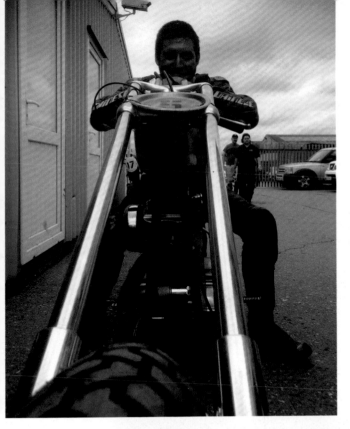

At Dirt Quake on the Krazy Horse Harley chopper.

Having a quick word with Carl Fogarty before the racing started.

Bonneville, what a place.

Matt Markstaller is in the blue T-shirt, James the MoTeC man is in the black shirt and Ed the engine man (with the grey beard) is stood next to me.

Me and Sal talking to Mike Cook, the father of Bonneville, in Carmen's Black and White Bar, Wendover.

At Bonneville, Triumph laid on some camper vans for their photographers, sponsors, the team and the TV lot to use. Some guests of Triumph turned up and broke the golden rule of no number twos in the camper van, so someone put up a sign on the camper van saying MEDIA ONLY. It was only a matter of time before I made my own for the TV lot's camper van door.

We took the Transit to Bonneville to see what it could do, but it didn't get up to the speeds that the TV lot hoped it would.

My sticker, and a lot of bullet holes on the famous sign that tells

for the Martek and the wall of death bike. They had a really nicely done Kawasaki Zed and a Suzuki Katana on show there. There was a lot of cool stuff, and I don't know why *Sideburn* never did another Rollerburn, but the next idea they came up with was Dirt Quake.

Gary at *Sideburn* had been racing dirt track for a few years. He'd noticed that people were nervous of getting involved, and he wanted to show that it was easy to get into. He came up with the idea of putting on a dirt track race on a proper track, with all the insurance and medical cover of a regular race but open to people who'd never raced before. He also made sure they could enter on just about whatever bike they had. He didn't want the kind of bikes that could easily compete in other races, because there was nothing stopping those folk from competing week in, week out somewhere in the country if they put their mind to it. So at Dirt Quake they have race classes like Inappropriate Road Bike and Street Tracker (for bikes that look a bit like proper race bikes but are road legal). There is also a class for women and a chopper class.

The first Dirt Quake I raced in was at King's Lynn in 2014. There had been a couple before that, and I'd read the reports in *Sideburn*. Then, when Gary asked if I wanted to race a Harley chopper supplied by Krazy Horse, I was well up for it – and it was a free weekend, so …

The Harley I raced wasn't too chopped, but it definitely wasn't a race bike, and I won on it. The next year Krazy

Horse changed it, going for a bit of a truck theme with it. The bike had longer forks, tassels on the end of the handlebars, those chrome silhouettes of women that truck drivers used to bolt to their mud flaps, and exhausts that kicked straight up at the air and had flappers on the top, like some American trucks have. I won on it again. This would be my third year.

Dirt Quake is a two-day event, held over Friday night and Saturday. It's run with the help of the club that run the British dirt track championship, the DTRA (Dirt Track Riders Association). They run their regular races on a Friday night, with the daft Dirt Quake stuff on Saturday. I hadn't ridden dirt track for ages, so I entered the Friday night races too.

The DTRA has a few different classes: Pro, for the fastest riders; Restricted is one class below; Rookies is for beginners; Vintage and Thunderbike. The last of these is the championship for bikes that have steel frames and older engines – not the modern 450 motocross engines that are the fastest bikes out there – as the Thunderbikes are not old enough to be considered vintage. The right man on a good Thunderbike could still give the best 450 a run for its money, though.

I entered two classes, Pro and Thunderbike. I took three bikes, my modern Honda CRF450 that I'd raced at the Superprestigio, Marc Márquez's indoor dirt track race in Barcelona; a KTM, which is another modern 450, but

I didn't end up riding it; and my Honda CR500, which I bought from John Roeder, an American ex-serviceman who still lives in England. The CR500 is a mish-mash of all different parts, with a 1980s 500 cc two-stroke engine from a legendary motocrosser at the heart of it. The early CR500 engines are known for being vicious, and mine is an early one, with the longer stroke. I don't know why a longer-stroke two-stroke motor would be more vicious, but it probably isn't down to just the stroke. It'll have something to do with the porting too.

When I was 12 or 13 my mate Aaron Ash somehow got hold of a Maico 490, a massive two-stroke motocross bike. Along with our friend Mark 'Shorty' Nichols, we would ride it around the fields and gravel pits. It scared the shit out of me. It was the only experience I'd had of big single-cylinder two-strokes, but I'd heard boys talk of CR500s. They were the next generation, liquid-cooled and reed-valved, and the CR500s blew the Maicos away.

The CR500 had sat in my kitchen all year, since the DTRA round at Dirt Quake in 2015. The night before the race I got the wheel starter out and said to Sharon, 'If it starts I'll take it tomorrow.' It struck up right away. There were a few bolts missing, because it vibrates like buggery, and it needed a bit of tidying up. Basically, it's alright – Tim Neave used to race it and won the DTRA Thunderbike championship on it – but I want it spot on. There's a load of bits I'd like to do to it, but I'd done bugger all. And all I did on the Thursday night was tighten a few bolts, oil the chain and wash it. But the experience of racing it again has made me keen to get it exactly how I want it. I'm not slagging it off, but I want it to be more me. It doesn't need a lot of money spending on it, just time.

I raced the 450 in the Pro class with the fast lads like Ade Collins, Alan Birtwistle and Ollie Brindley and did shit. In the DTRA you have three heat races, in each of the classes you race, to try to qualify for the finals. I was that rusty, I was just getting the hang of it by the end of the night, but I wasn't bothered. I'd have been better off just riding the CR500 in both classes, and I could have done that. They're so different to each other, the old two-stroke and the modern 450 two-stroke, and the 500 is actually easier to ride, which I never would have thought. The two-stroke is a bit lighter than the modern Honda, and the power isn't all or nothing, as you'd expect a two-stroke to be. It pulls from low revs and is dead usable. The thing that isn't very user-friendly is starting it. It hasn't got a kickstart, which makes it hard to start.

I qualified for the Thunderbike final, but then I stalled the CR in the holding area to go out for the final, and I couldn't get it bump-started. I had a wheel starter with me, but I was holding everyone up, so I just waved to say, Don't wait, go without me.

Sharon and I were going to sleep in the van, but I had three bikes – the two Hondas and the KTM 450 – the wheel starter, tool box and the dog, so there was no room. We didn't have to sign on till 11 the next day, so we drove home and did it in an hour and a half without going mad.

I was up early and did a few things with the Martek, the bike I raced at Pikes Peak, half hoping I could get on a track day at Cadwell that Robspeed, the local Grimsby bike shop, were running the following week. I wasn't sure if I'd make it, and I didn't. Then we set off back to King's Lynn to see what I'd be racing.

After winning the chopper class two years on the trot, I told Paul, the boss of Krazy Horse, that if I was going to do it again they should make it harder for me. He just laughed. By now, Krazy Horse had been a big part of the wall of death, because they'd built the Indians, and also the Transit for the Nevada Open Road Challenge. They really went to town with the Harley.

When we were in Vegas, doing the van thing, Paul wasn't making a big deal about the bike, but he said, 'Some boys I know in Sweden are making us a frame and we'll use some 22-inch over forks.' He explained that it meant the forks were 22 inches, or 56 centimetres, longer than the ones in the standard Harley Sportster. I knew it would be interesting, but it was hard for someone like me, who isn't that into choppers, to know what forks that are 22 inches longer than standard would look like. I reckoned it would be alright, but nothing prepared me for what it looked like when I saw it at the track.

If you saw this 1200 cc Harley being pushed into a custom show you'd think it would have a chance of winning a prize. It was wild-looking. The frame and petrol tank were bare metal, but the bike was well built, everything really well machined, all the wires and cables well routed. At past Dirt Quakes, the Krazy Horse bikes I'd raced looked daft on purpose. The first year, the petrol tank had been left to go rusty on the outside, the following year it was painted all different colours with spots of aerosol paint, and they looked good, but nothing like this. It was impressive.

I like the whole event. The wall of death was up in the middle of the track. I'd visited Ken Fox two weeks before, at an American car show in Tatton Park, because I hadn't seen him since the Channel 4 wall of death thing. The Fox family run two walls, and it was Ken's eldest son Luke, his family and crew at Dirt Quake. I thought I might have a go on the wall, but I never got round to it.

I like the people who race. My mate Shorty and his missus, Hannah, come to watch. He loves his bikes, but you wouldn't get him to any other motorbike event. Me, Shorty and Butch were the first of us Kirmo lot to go on a road trip to a foreign track. We went to Cartagena in southern Spain for a few track days, with a stop in Benidorm on the way home to see Sticky Vicky's notorious performance.

The race is held at King's Lynn speedway track, and the pits are only made to comfortably house 16 speedway bikes. For Dirt Quake there are nearly a hundred bikes crammed in. We took Nigel, and he wasn't bothered about the noise – it's all he's had since he was a nipper – but he was a bit miserable. He was going through a lazy phase. I was parked up next to a bloke called Vince and his missus, Holly. I'd seen him the year before, a cool bloke.

Dirt Quake attracts the right sort of people. It's just lads and lasses into all sorts of stuff. There were some cool cars parked up outside. A 1950s Dodge Coronet pulling a trailer with an old Triumph and an even older Harley on it. I got talking to another bloke in the chopper class. I had my John Deere body warmer on, and he said, 'Oh, I'm just mucking about with an old John Deere TVO engine.' That's a type of diesel engine that you start running with petrol then swap to diesel when it gets hot. It was interesting, not motorbike talk, though I'm happy talking about motorbikes too. Anyway, the following week he sent me a letter written in the neatest handwriting, telling me about this van he's converted with a six-cylinder Mercedes engine in it, saying he's got 450 horsepower out of it. He's definitely not a messer, because his handwriting was so neat.

Gregory, the Scania man from France, was there too. I'd first met him when I raced at Le Mans. He had come over with some French mates of his, and he brought me a load of Scania stuff, like he always does, so I gave him a Tyco TAS jacket that only the team get given. He's quite well up at Scania, so he's good for information, and he was telling me a bit about a new model due to be released later this year.

A few people wanted stuff signing, but not enough for Brian the Chimp to make an appearance. (Brian is my inner chimp, thanks to Dr Steve Peters' book *The Chimp Paradox*.) Fiddy, from the British helmet company Davida, gave me a couple of TT scrapbooks to read between races. They were dead good, and there was even a bit about Freddy Frith, the late motorcycle world champion from Grimsby. He was Grand Prix 350 world champion, back when that was an important class, in 1949. He won all five grands prix that year, and he was one of the few racers who won TTs either side of the Second World War.

Carl Fogarty was there too. He was working for an insurance company that sponsors Dirt Quake, and they'd invited him along. He was racing a trick modern Triumph street tracker, so he wasn't in my class. We said hello, but didn't have much time to talk. I knew him a bit because I'd interviewed him at his house for *Performance Bikes* magazine years ago. He's a legend.

Then it was time to race the chopper. You'd look at it and you wouldn't even think it would get around a corner on a speedway track, but it was nowhere near as bad as it looked. I was surprised. I wasn't overthinking any tactics – just turn the throttle and see how we go. The back end would step out, but it wasn't as predictable as the Harley I'd raced the year before. On the previous chopper, which was nowhere near as long, I had the confidence to hold it in a drift, but the back end of the long bike felt like it snapped out of line more quickly and less predictably. When it let go, it let go. Strangely, I didn't have one front-end moment. I thought it would be worse because it had no weight on it. I could see the line on the track where the grip was, and I'd aim for that, but the front end was that far in front of me I had to make the decision about where I wanted the front wheel much earlier. If I didn't get it right, the front tyre was in the loose stuff, but it still wasn't washing out. The bike understeered, but it never folded; it just pushed wide, in a very progressive slide. It wasn't like a normal dirt track bike, where the front end goes suddenly and you have to support the bike on your foot. The chopper's front wheel seemed to be sliding nearly all the way through the corner, but by putting a bit of weight through my left foot – I had a steel shoe strapped to the bottom of my boot – it was half-controllable.

Overtakes were fun. If you're up against someone of a similar speed and you're both racing normal bikes, you edge up the inside of them at first, hoping they'll leave enough room for you to come through, and not turn sharply in front of you. Because dirt track bikes only have a back brake, and the back end will skid if you brake too hard, overtaking isn't just a case of getting up alongside someone and block passing them on the brakes. Do that and you risk sliding off and taking both of you out. The chopper was different. I could show them a front wheel and they knew what was coming three weeks later. It was like a warning shot. I still needed full commitment, but I was laughing.

I won my first heat race, and I didn't think it was going to be that easy. For the second race I went on the back row and still won, on the last corner of the last lap. The big V-twin was accelerating well down the straights. I'd brake in a straight line and then tip it in. I wasn't drifting it in like I would on a dirt tracker.

In the final I was a bit too hard on the throttle on the loose dirt and got the back end out. It let a rider called Odgie come past on an old 650 BSA. He was 62 years old and was doing well. I could've put a pass on him, but it might have been a bit hard. I was a bit annoyed I didn't win, but I thought the bike was great. Paul Krazy Horse came up after the race and said, 'We've succeeded! You said make it harder, and we did.'

It reminded me that Dirt Quake is not the kind of place where you can turn up and try to be cool. A load of French nutters were there dressed as the Simpsons. There was another French lad who came over on his own, in a people carrier with a Yamaha 500 in the back. We were parked next to each other, and I offered him a sandwich and he made me a coffee. He raced at Dirt Quake, and that night he was getting the late boat to Calais, so he could go kitesurfing off the French coast the next day, then back to work in Paris on Monday morning. He said he cleaned windows on skyscrapers in the summer and went to Alpe d'Huez to work as a ski instructor in the winter. I thought, You cool bastard!

Something else happened the other day that made me think of Dirt Quake. I got in the works van and Capital FM was on, so Belty must have been in it last. Capital FM is more Radio 1 than Radio 1. Everything is super and awesome and 'like that!', with every sentence having an upward inflection at the end of it. Radio 1 is setting the scene for how the youth of the nation is meant to look and act – what's trending, who is tweeting this and following that. Capital FM is trying so hard to be like Radio 1, but trying too hard. I was listening to it for half an hour, just fascinated by what they thought was worth saying. Some of the music was alright, but I wondered if I was so uncool that I couldn't find one thing they were talking about the least bit interesting. I'm not in that world, and I don't want to be in it. I'm not against Twitter, but I don't want it ramming down my throat. Some of the motorbike world is similar, where people feel they have to keep up with the Joneses. It annoys me now that people have loud exhausts on their motorbikes. I think, You've only fitted that to be seen and heard. But I've got bikes with noisy exhausts. Another example is someone saying to me, 'Your brother can do this lap time round Cadwell.' And I thought, Does that make him a better person? You couldn't find a nicer person than our Stu and it wasn't him saying it, but it made me wonder why this bloke seemed to be judging him differently because he was two seconds a lap quicker than he used to be. I was in that scene when I was in the British championship, before the whole laptop, Scarborough, going to Ireland period of my life. And I saw that if you could do a particular lap time, you could move up the social hierarchy. Dirt Quake is nothing like that. That's why I like it.

CHAPTER 16

You need a lot of power to run the dribble bar

I SOUND LIKE a right flash bastard when I think how many vehicles I've ended up with. I made a list and it looks daft, but I've still got the first motorbike I ever had on the road, my Kawasaki AR50. I don't sell much, and others have come with deals. When I was planning this book, Andy

Spellman thought it might be interesting for me to talk about them and how I came to own some of them.

Other than the AR50, the vehicle I've owned the longest is my 1972 Saab 96. I nearly swapped it years ago. A mate was going to buy it, because I wanted a Volkswagen Variant Fastback, but he didn't in the end and I'm glad. It's matt black with hot rod flames and a fake leopard-skin interior.

I have the world's fastest Volvo Amazon, which I bought from Sweden in 2011. It has a modern six-cylinder Volvo T6 turbo engine, and it's the fastest thing I've ever been in. Other than my Transit, it's the vehicle I use the most. I bet I've done 5,000 miles in it, and I took it to Lincoln on the way to do some filming. Nige was in the back, and I don't know why, but he hates it. It might be the howl from the turbo that sets him off. Sharon says she doesn't like it either, but she does really. When she's in, she'll say, 'Go on, then,' encouraging me to give it some.

It's originally a 1968 estate, but Mattias Vöcks, the bloke who built it, has changed nearly everything. He's an engineer at Swedish supercar manufacturer Koenigsegg. I normally want to change or improve stuff other people have built to make it my own, but I'm happy to leave the Amazon, though I have spent a lot of time spannering it. It's broken down twice, and I've had to fit a new crank to it.

It runs on E85, fuel that is 85 per cent ethanol, 15 per cent unleaded. You used to be able to buy it from pumps in Britain. It's good for this car, because it's very knock resistant, meaning it's not prone to detonation (also known as knock or pinking), so you can use loads of turbo boost, but you also need to run a lot of ignition advance because the ethanol is very slow-burning when it's in the combustion chamber. To make the most of this, you light that fuel a lot earlier, so when it reaches its optimum flame path, the piston is in the right place. You light it 60 degrees before top dead centre. You might run a naturally aspirated engine 25 degrees before top dead centre, at the most. You also have to burn more E85 than petrol, so it uses 30 per cent more fuel. E85 has a similar cooling effect to nitromethane, which drag-race engines run on. Top fuel drag cars are the quickest accelerating things on the planet, reaching 100 mph in 0.8 seconds, and they can burn 35 litres of fuel in a single quarter-mile run. A family car, doing 50 miles to the gallon, would cover 385 miles on the same amount of fuel. It takes 1,000 horsepower just to run a top fuel dragster's supercharger, but once the supercharger is spinning it helps the engine produce 10,000 horsepower. They've only just managed to measure how much power to fuel a dragster makes using strain gauges.

Top fuel cars are fitted with aluminium conrods. To light the fuel they use spark and detonation (by that I mean the mixture explodes purely under pressure – it's 'pinking', which is bad for a regular engine). There is so much fuel in the combustion chamber that these motors are on the verge of hydraulic locking when they're at top dead centre. The piston compresses the mixture, but because it's almost liquid it can only compress it so much, unlike the more gaseous cloud of air and petrol in the regular engine. The aluminium conrods are chosen, instead of steel or titanium conrods, because the alloy acts as a shock absorber.

I've gone off track here. Mattias, who I bought the Amazon from, built it to run on E85, and I've left it how he built it. I could change the ignition timing and run less boost, so it could run on super unleaded, but it would run too hot. I'll just keep using loads of the really expensive fuel when I use the Amazon. The car is good for having a mad half-hour every now and then, but I'm not interested in taking it on track days or anything like that.

I don't know what it is about me and Swedish vehicles, Scanias, Volvos, Saabs … They all do a squillion miles, they're proper built things and I've ended up with another old Volvo, a 1965 P1800. I never thought about these until I bought the Amazon. In Mattias's shed was a P1800 that had a more modern T5 engine in it and nice wheels. When I got home I started looking at P1800s. Everyone associates them with the 1960s Roger Moore spy programme, *The Saint*, but I'd never seen it. At the back of my mind was the thought that I'd like a good usable one. Bill Gordon from Red Torpedo, the clothing company that has been sponsoring me for years, visited me and I took him out in the Amazon, and when we got back he asked if I'd rather have a P1800 than the money his company owed me. Spellman found a dead tidy blue one that had been restored years ago. It's one of the last ones running on carbs. The later ones were fuel-injected, and I don't want anything with 1960s fuel injection.

Somehow, I also ended up with a knackered Mk3 Volkswagen Polo. I met Mad Adrian in the early days of racing the TT, when he and his mate would ride over from Manchester on their mopeds. He's a good lad. He started working at Dounreay nuclear power station, and he was travelling back to Manchester every weekend. The Polo was his only transport, and when it shit itself I lent him the money so he could buy a Golf from my mate Jim Andrews, a car dealer. Mad Adrian ended up giving me his knackered Polo instead of paying me interest on the loan. It sat outside my house for over a year upsetting the neighbours. I had a mad idea that I'd leave it looking rough, but fit a Powertec V8 in it, one of those engines Radical use that's made from one-and-a-half Hayabusas, but I never did.

When Sharon moved over from Ireland she needed a car, so I thought I'd get the Polo running. I bought an engine from Hector Neill, the owner of the TAS BMW team (TAS stands for Temple Auto Salvage), and brought it home in my van from the 2015 North West 200. A few months later I was supposed to be doing a thing at a show with Dainese, but the flights got cancelled or summat and I ended up back home at dinnertime with no plans, so I decided to fit the replacement engine in the Polo. I borrowed an engine hoist from a garage down the road and took one driveshaft off, so I could disconnect the gearbox and move it round to the side to get the engine out. I swapped it on the driveway. Eventually, Sharon got fed up with the Polo's doors not locking, and even though it had just passed its MOT, she wanted something newer, so I bought a Land Rover Defender 90 for her. I'd always liked them, but I never drive it because I'm always in the Transit.

Another car I've ended up with more recently was bought from Uncle Rodders (who isn't my uncle). He owned a 1975 Pontiac Firebird for 15 or 20 years, and I'd always seen it in his shed when I called round there. He's helped me out loads over the years, so I said to him, 'Let me have that Pontiac and I'll get it finished for you.' He came back to me and said, 'Thanks, but you won't do it like I'd want.' He wanted it rat-look, but I didn't want to do it like that, so he sold me it for £1,800 and it's become a future project. The goal of that Firebird is to scare me more than the Amazon does. I've never had the horizon coming towards me as fast as it seems to when I'm driving that Volvo, and that includes riding a Superbike at the Isle of Man. So I want 2,000 horsepower out of the Firebird. You can put a Chevy LS1 V8 in them. That's a big cc, pushrod V8, and I'd put a supercharger on it. I think I want the supercharger poking so high through the bonnet that you can hardly see past it, but I'll decide on that when I get my eye in on the job. At the moment I'm thinking stripped-out interior: roll cage; driver's seat; big eff-off rev counter; big eff-off oil light; temperature gauge. A bit *Death Proof*.

Before the Firebird I might have to finish another big project I've just landed myself with. Mark Walker, who was one of the founders of Martek and was asked to be the technical advisor on my wall of death bike, bought a Ford Escort RS Cosworth years ago, the one with the whale tail on it. Then he cut it up to make a P100-style pick-up. Cosworths have always been worth a lot, so I don't know what made him do it, but I like his style. Mark had space-framed the whole chassis, but like Uncle Rodders, it was a case of, 'It'll be done next year, it'll be done next year ...' Finally, he admitted he'll never finish it, and he was looking to get rid of it. I'd known about it for years and saw there was a deal to be done, so I had it. It's a bare shell, no engine, no interior. I think I'm going to put an EcoBoost V6, the same engine as the Transit, in it.

Talking of Transits, I have the Transit Custom, FT13 AFK, which I raced in Nevada, but we've covered that.

I also have the grey Transit L2 H2 that I ended up with in a deal with Ford for going to a couple of their events. That's the vehicle I use the most.

I haven't finished yet. I bought a Fendt tractor, because I liked the idea of having a finger in another pie. I chose the German tractor because all the boys round here had said it was the Rolls-Royce of the farm world, and I'm sure they are a fantastic tractor, but I take as I find, and I had nothing but trouble with mine. In the year I had the Fendt, Tim Coles drove it for us during the day and I did odd nights in it, while it was used for shit-spreading on local farms. Sharon didn't show any signs of being keen to do that.

I wanted rid of it, and I lost a few quid when I traded it in, but it had worked hard for a year. I replaced it with the John Deere 7310R. The John Deere and the Fendt are both big tractors, and you need a lot of horsepower for the shit-spreading job, because you've got nearly 40 tons to shift: 11 or 12 tons of tractor, 8 tons of trailer and then 15 tons of shit on board, plus you need a lot of power to run the dribble bar.

The Fendt did a bit of leading work, when it was wheat and barley harvest time, towing a trailer to transport the harvest from the combine to the grain stores. It did some silage work, too, but the Fendt was a monster, and it couldn't go on the tatie job. Whatever wheels we thought about putting on it, we couldn't get it to fit between the rows of potatoes, which are planted in rows at set widths, so the tractor was missing out on some good work. A local potato firm rents a tractor every year for drilling the seeds, and the John Deere is suitable, so I'm hoping it will pick up that work too.

The John Deere is an ex-demo 2016 model and it pays for itself, pays Tim a wage and earns a quid or two on top, and I always had a soft spot for John Deere stuff. I'll always have the truck job, but there'll come a day when the TV job dries up, and I don't want all my eggs in one basket. When that happens I'll be alright. If you need me, I'll be shit-spreading.

Motorbikes ... I mentioned the old AR50 I used to go to work on as an apprentice. The other bike I've owned for years, on and off, is a 2004 Suzuki GSX-R1000. It's the last road race bike I owned myself, until 2015, because after that I was riding for teams and using their bikes. I came seventh in the Isle of Man Senior TT in my first ever year on this Suzuki, and it is the bike Uncle Rodders cast a new subframe for so I could get the riding position I wanted. A few years ago Spellman tracked it down and bought it as a surprise for me, because he knew it was the race bike that meant the most to me. He wouldn't tell me how much he paid for it, so that means whoever sold him it had his eye out, but Spellman said it wasn't about the money. It has the original fairings, but the wrong brakes on it now, so I want to put it back to how it was when I had it when I get time.

Another road race bike I have is the Smiths Triumph 675. I bought it in 2015 to go racing on. I needed a Supersport bike because when TAS swapped from Suzuki to BMW they didn't have one for me to race, as BMW don't build one. I bought this trick Triumph and only used it for one practice session at the Ulster before the crash made me have a rethink about road racing.

As part of the deal with Smiths I also got a standard road-legal Triumph Daytona 675R Carbon Edition. It's brand new, without a mile on it. I have no interest in it as it is, and I don't know what to do with it. Nik, the marketing man from Triumph whose idea it was for me to ride the land speed record streamliner, reckons I should store it as an investment. It might be a Nürburgring test machine.

I've got the wall of death Rob North and the Bimota VDue I wrote about in *When You Dead, You Dead*. It's a fuel-injected 500 cc two-stroke V-twin. I loved the idea of it, but it's shit. Oh, and the Pikes Peak Martek and the dirt trackers I mentioned in the Dirt Quake chapter. There's a Harley, too, a real rare-looking thing I bought from Andy Spellman. When it comes to bikes he wants to get on and ride it, whereas custom bikes need a lot of looking after and fettling. You can't leave them for a month and expect them to be perfect, like you can a modern stock bike. You've got to check the oil and keep on top of them. Spellman's a very clever man, very good with cameras, but he didn't know how to check the oil on this Harley, so buying it was more of a mercy mission. It was like seeing a pit bull tied up in a garden, unloved and neglected. I had to give it a good home, but it's not for me. I went out on it once and it nearly put me off motorbikes. There are so many trick bits on it, but it's bloody noisy and the riding position is all wrong for me.

My latest bike is a 1988 Yamaha TZR250 Reverse Cylinder that I bought off Stewart, one of Moody's drivers, who needed some money in a hurry. It's a trick thing and rare. They were never officially imported into Britain. It's far from mint, but it's original. I've got the standard pipes for it. It makes 65 horsepower, so it's quick and sounds the bollocks. I don't know when I'm ever going to use it, though.

That's it for motorbikes, but my Rolls-Royce Spitfire engine is up in the Grampian Transport Museum, who are mates of Francis Dungait, my mountain-bike mate who I wrote about in *When You Dead, You Dead*, after he shocked me and Sal by smacking Nigel the dog on his snout. Chris Kelly of Keltruck wanted a sticker on my helmet years ago, and I swapped it for a Scania 144 530 V8 engine. It looks like a complete engine, but it's a show motor with no valve gear in it. The Scania V8 is famous in the world I'm in, and they put the V8 logo on everything, they're that proud of it. The engine just sat in a corner at Moody's, but I'm keeping it because I've worked on them since I was 12 years old.

Lawnmowers are another thing that I've ended up with loads of. I have a brand new Hayter for my grass at home, because my lawn is rubbish, and I've got an old Atco, from the early seventies, unrestored, electric start with a bowling green roller on it. It's a nice old lawnmower. And I swapped a turbo trainer for another nice Atco, from the 1950s. I just like them.

Bicycles are something else again. I'm building a steel-framed Rourke with Shimano Di2 electronic gear shifters, all the Hope bits, Fox suspension. I have another Rourke, a single-speed, which I ride to work on. The land-speed bike and the Salsa Fargo Tour Divide bike are both on display in my mate's bike shop.

I have a lot of bikes made by the British company Orange. In some sort of order I have: 322 downhill bike; Clockwork hardtail; 29-inch Gyro 24-hour race bike; Five mountain bike; Alpine 160 26-inch that Hope gave me; new Alpine 160 with Di2 electronic gear set on it; RX9 cyclocross bike and Carb-O carbon road bike, but I've loaned it to a young lad, Ben Neave, Tim and Tom's little brother, to ride. And that's it.

I look at the list of stuff I've got and wonder, How have I ended up with all this? I don't need it, I know that, but I like all this shit.

CHAPTER 17

I felt sorry for him, because I stunk the day I met him

NEVER HAS SO much piss been sent into the wind. Trying to break the world record for human-powered watercraft was another project for the 2016 *Speed* series. The series was four programmes long and split down the middle, half human-powered, me being the human, and half involving big turbo engines.

The record we were chasing belongs to Mark Drela from the American university MIT, the Massachusetts Institute of Technology. His speed was 18.5 knots, the equivalent of 21.3 mph. It doesn't sound that fast, does it? But Drela is not a messer. He's a professor specialising in the aeronautical and astronautical side of things, with a bit of fluid dynamics chucked in for good measure.

I looked him up, and the MIT's website has a page on him describing what he's up to. Here's a bit of it: 'Current research involves development of computational algorithms for the prediction of 2D and 3D external flows about aerodynamic bodies. Subsonic, transonic, and supersonic flow regimes are being considered. Most of the work centers on viscous/inviscid coupling schemes in conjunction with direct Newton solution methods. Two- and three-dimensional integral boundary layer formulations are also being developed for modeling viscous regions.'

Exactly. But we had some brains involved in our attempt too. Lincoln University had set their students a project to design a potential record breaker, and they'd got in touch with North One to see if there was any interest in working together. One of Lincoln's professors, Ron Bickerton, was our main contact. He's in his sixties, with a long grey ponytail, and lives on a boat when he's working at the university.

For the first day of filming, we met on Ron's boat at Burton Waters, near Lincoln. He told us what the students had been up to and showed us footage of the current record being set.

When I thought of human-powered watercraft, I pictured a swan pedalo on a boating lake. And it sounded like what we were doing was building a glorified pedalo. I hadn't had that much experience with pedalos, but I'd had enough. I'd hired one in Croatia once. It had a slide on the front. It was trick.

Mark Drela's record breaker was called the *Decavitator*, and it was a pedal-powered watercraft with a big propeller on the back like one of those airboats they have in the swamps of Florida. The YouTube clip of it in action didn't look that impressive, initially, then I kept watching it and realised that Drela, who was not only the designer, but was also pedalling it, was licking on.

Ron was the driving force of our project. He explained that he had this man involved, and that man doing this, and that the students had all these great ideas. As time went on I got the feeling they were full of great ideas and big words, but after a while it seemed to me that next to bugger all was actually happening. I'd had involvement with universities before in the previous *Speed* series, and the ones that stand out the most are the projects we'd done with Sheffield Hallam University, brilliant stuff like the gravity racer, which did 85.61 mph down Mont Ventoux (before Brian the Chimp had a furry hand in crashing it) and the 83.49 mph sledge. I felt the Lincoln side fell down when it actually came to turning the great words that were falling out of their mouths into action.

The *Speed* programmes often involve some sort of sports science along with the engineering challenges, and this one was no different. As part of the programme I visited Lincoln University to do a load of dyno tests on a static exercise bike, linked up to a load of monitors. We wanted to make sure I could put out the wattage they reckoned we needed to produce for the machine to break the record.

Another thing North One are good at doing is getting high-profile experts to give me some advice. For this programme we had a couple of knights who have won ten Olympic gold medals between them. First, I had a day with Sir Chris Hoy in Lincoln University, then I went sailing with Sir Ben Ainslie. The cycling legend was brought in to suggest some training for a bit of TV bullshit, and what a lovely bloke. I felt a bit sorry for him, because I stunk the day I met him. I was training for the Tour Divide, and I'd set off at daft o'clock in the morning to cycle the long way to meet him at Lincoln University. I hadn't had a proper wash for three days. I don't get washed that often if I'm at work – what's the point if I'm not that caked up? And I was wearing waterproofs, so it was a bit boil-in-the-bag. I could even smell myself, so it must have been bad. He didn't say anything, though, because he's a polite man.

It was worked out how many watts I theoretically needed to put out and for how long to have a crack at breaking the record. I did manage to make enough power, and for long enough, in the lab tests, and during the day Chris Hoy came out with some interesting stuff that wasn't really anything to do with the programme. He explained that he was never a natural, and that kids who are thought of as naturals at school age are often winning mainly because they're bigger and stronger, having developed earlier than most of their competition. These kids get used to winning, but when the other kids' physiques build and strength increases, they catch up, the 'natural' kids start losing more than they win, and that's when they pack in. Chris said he had to work at it, and he reckons it's the kids who never had success, the ones who it didn't come easy for, but they kept working at it, who are the ones to put your money on. He was one of them.

He's the same height as me, but he's a much bigger build, even though he said he'd lost 4 kilograms, over half a stone, since he retired from racing. He gave me some interval training tips to increase my maximum power, but nothing that would help me with endurance. I think I am what I am when it comes to endurance.

Chris Hoy came to track cycling from racing BMX. I asked if he knew Dave Maw, my mate Jonty's brother who I mentioned in *When You Dead, You Dead*. Dave was three-time world champion and sadly died at a young age in a car crash. Chris Hoy said, 'Dave Maw! Do you know Dave Maw?' I explained that I didn't, but I knew the family. He was a year younger than Chris, but he was winning more.

Multi-million-pound America's Cup racing yachts are designed to be hydrofoils, like our pedalo, so the TV lot decided that it would be good telly to get me out on one of these cutting-edge boats. They sorted it for me to spend a day with the best, Sir Ben Ainslie and his whole crew.

It was another example of TV bullshit, to be out on this massive multi-million-pound racing yacht to see how a hydrofoil worked, but I wasn't complaining, because again, what an honour and opportunity. I knew the name Ben Ainslie from hearing it on the radio, but I didn't know anything about him. He's won medals at five consecutive Olympic games, including four golds. He's also won 11 sailing world championships, and he's been awarded an MBE, OBE and CBE and been knighted. Everyone on that boat had massive respect for him, and they were all hard bastards.

It was a brilliant experience. That crew are as fit as. When you see them with their hand on the handles of a winch, spinning it like hell, it's what they call grinding, and they're powering everything on the boat. The rules say you are not allowed to have any stored energy on the boat, so it all must be man-powered, and that's what the grinders do. I did a bit of it and it's bloody hard work. All the controls are mirrored on either side of the boat, and the way it's leaning determines which controls the crew use.

We sailed out of Portsmouth towards the Isle of Wight, and I was mucking about grinding for a bit, then they did proper race simulations. The boats lick along at 40-odd knots, which is pretty fast on water. I found out that whoever wins the America's Cup decides when the next one is, where it is and what the rules are. There are only ever six boats, including the previous winner. The next one is 2017.

The budget of an America's Cup team is massive. The team I was with, the Land Rover BAR team, had something like a £150 million budget. It makes MotoGP look like club racing at Mallory Park.

Ainslie is one of the most respected men in the sailing game. He was brought in as the tactician of the struggling Oracle team at the last America's Cup, in 2012–13, after the Oracle team had lost four of the first five races, and helped them win it. From what I'm told no one had ever made a comeback like it. He's very posh, not a messer, but all the crew were gritty bastards. We were out on the water from nine till two, then they had a training session, with a personal trainer, after that. It was all very structured.

I had a tour of the headquarters and saw they have an office full of 20 people, a lot of them ex-Formula One, most doing boat design for the team. You'd have to see it to believe it, because I've never seen anything like it.

Back at pedalo-design headquarters in Lincoln I saw the fancy carbon-fibre catamaran hull that had been made. The record was set using an air propeller, but the Lincoln lot decided to use a water propeller. The design of it was called a highly skewed, asymmetric prop. It was developed for submarines because it's quieter than previous propellers. I was told that this design was also more efficient, converting more of their energy into forward motion. Ron explained all this to me and it sounded good. I was convinced.

The catamaran hull would also have hydrofoils attached. These work like a plane's wing, but in water. The foils produce lift, at a certain speed, pushing the hull up and out of the water, reducing the drag and increasing the potential speed. Ron also had an idea to fill the centre between the two hulls, so when the hydrofoils lifted the boat out of the water there would be a ground effect helping to keep it up on the hydrofoils. This idea was used by the Ekranoplan, Russia's experimental ground-effect aircraft. The one I'd heard of was the KM, an enormous Ekranoplan that was first tested in 1966. It's the oddest-looking plane, with stubby, broad square wings, a massive tail wing and eight jet engines, mounted four on each side just behind the cockpit, with another two jet engines on the tail, so ten in total. American spy satellites spotted it at a test site, and after first thinking it was a half-built plane, waiting for the rest of its wings to be bolted on, they worked out what it could be and nicknamed it the Caspian Sea Monster. You look at this thing and think, Mother Mary! It was a sort of seaplane, but it only flew 20 feet above the water or ice. It was so big, and could carry so much cargo, that it needed something for the air beneath its wings to push against to be able to fly. The idea was that it could transport more weight more efficiently than traditional transport planes of the time, and it could. It was also harder to spot with radar, which was useful in those Cold War times. The Russians built loads of different prototypes, but the whole Ekranoplan idea didn't come to anything in the end. The Caspian Sea Monster was tested until 1980, when it crashed and sunk. I was finding all this fascinating, but I still wasn't convinced that the boat being built would be as successful as it needed to be.

The first test of our boat was at Burton Waters, where we'd met Ron to hear his plan at the start of filming. The pedalling gear wasn't fitted to the boat yet, so we towed it with another boat to try to prove the theory of the hull. It tried coming up on the hydrofoils, which were on something like four-foot-tall stilts, but they kept breaking. They were reinforced, we'd try again and they'd break again.

Once the pedalling gear was fitted, we returned to test the boat again. The asymmetric prop had to spin at 3,000 rpm, so it needed a gearbox to convert my pedalling cadence to that huge rpm, but the gearbox was only small so that kept breaking too. Then the chain alignment was out, and it kept chucking the chain off.

It all seemed to be going tits, when a couple of Ron's former students, Jez and Simon, who both worked for Siemens in Lincoln, got involved. Jez and Simon redesigned the gearbox, working in their sheds every night. They made it all work, but the concept was fundamentally flawed. Really they just shined the shit.

When we visited Ben Ainslie's America's Cup design office, we showed one of their designers photos of our boat and he wondered out loud, 'Why haven't you used an air prop? Why do you have two hulls instead of one?' We didn't really have an answer – it was what Ron and his students had decided.

James Woodroffe, one of North One TV's executive producers, took all this in and, when the Lincoln boat was looking like a shower of shit, he decided to put a plan B into action. He contacted a bloke called Mike, from down Bristol way, who designs and builds racing

Moths. These are small, single-hull sailing dinghies that use hydrofoils. James arranged for a single-hull boat with an air propeller to be built. If nowt else we could compare the two concepts. Mike was a real switched-on lad, younger than me, and he assembled his version of the potential record breaker in my back garden.

As the record-attempt day drew closer I met with the Lincoln lot at Burton Waters for extra tests when the cameras weren't there, because I was that into it. I'd been down a couple of nights after work and a couple of Sundays too – I don't want to just rock up on a filming day – but we were still way off the record. I would power this boat lying in a recumbent position, so legs out in front of me, lying back, not a regular cycling position, because it's more aerodynamic, but it wasn't making enough of a difference.

Time was running out. It was planned that I'd do a practice day, then go for the record over two consecutive days on Brayford Pool in the centre of Lincoln, but another spanner was thrown in the works, making me think that perhaps the whole thing was doomed. Brayford Pool was choked with thick weed that would wrap around the hydrofoils and the water propeller.

Both boats came, and Ron looked like he'd got the hump when the plan B boat turned up, so we prettied it up to say it was single hull versus twin hull and water prop versus air prop. And it was – there was no denying it. The Lincoln team's Ekranoplan idea never happened. They ran out of time to get it sorted.

We had nothing to lose so I gave it a go, attempting two runs with the Lincoln boat, but it went terrible, with loads of weed getting wrapped around the hydrofoils. Mike said the hydrofoils were so sensitive that one strand of weed could stop them working, and he didn't even bother unloading his plan B boat.

I did the two runs and it was back in the van and time to work out a plan. We found some clean water in a place called Carsington Water, near Derby, and headed there the next day with both boats.

We knew the Lincoln boat wasn't going to bother the record, but I gave it another go. In that boat the harder I pedalled the harder it seemed to get. The Carlos Fandango asymmetric prop was so hard to turn, and it was jarring me every time I turned the cranks. I could only get a cadence of 60, when I really needed twice that. It was knackering. I was the fittest I'd ever been, coming off the back of the Tour Divide, but this required a different kind of pedalling. It was cough-your-lungs-up-for-a-couple-of-minutes effort.

Then I had a go with plan B, and nothing broke or gave any bother, but it was slow.

Neither of them got up on their hydrofoils. The MIT boat, the *Decavitator*, used a ladder system of hydrofoils and it obviously worked. The fastest I went was 5.45

mph, about a quarter of what I needed to match the record. I don't even think Chris Hoy would be able to go four times as quick as me. A few people have tried to break Drela's record since 1991, and it still stands.

The effort, both plans A and B, was a failure, but it showed that the records we attempt and usually break during the filming of *Speed* are not easy, and failing every now and then never hurt anyone. With three or four other record attempts coming up before the end of the year, I was hoping that I wasn't going to make a habit of failing, though.

CHAPTER 18

I laughed and reminded her I wasn't here to go steady

ATTEMPTING TO BREAK the outright motorcycle land speed record had been on the cards since I flew out to see Matt Markstaller in April 2015. That one-night trip, to Portland, Oregon, had been sold to me as making sure

I could fit in the Triumph streamliner, because it was built with someone six inches shorter than me in mind. Markstaller is the hot rod builder and truck research and development engineer who had been paid by Triumph to build a motorcycle capable of breaking the land speed record, which at the time was 376.363 mph. I now realise that the trip was more of a job interview, with Matt making sure he wanted to work with me.

I must have said the right things, because the first record attempt was set to be in August 2015, but, as you already know, I broke my back, and Bonneville was flooded anyway. The Bonneville Salt Flats in Utah were formed when a prehistoric salt lake, 1,000-foot deep in places, dried up over hundreds of thousands of years, leaving all the salt and minerals that were suspended in the water to self-level and form a flat surface. People have raced cars on it since 1914, with regular annual speed meetings held there since the end of the Second World War. Now, weather permitting, there are three or four speed trial events, for cars and motorbikes, held there every year, and other private tests and record attempts on top of that.

The majority of the outright land speed records of all time have been set at Bonneville, but the car record is now so high, at 760.343 mph, that Bonneville isn't big enough for them to get up to speed and slow down, so they look for other deserts. The folk behind the British

Bloodhound SSC, which has a target speed of 1,000 mph, have prepared their own track in South Africa. Hundreds of racers still bring their hot rods and streamliners to see what they can do, with no dream or possibility of setting the outright car record. They're looking for class records, personal bests or to break their own limits.

If the salt is in good condition Bonneville is just about long enough for motorcycles to reach 400 mph, though nobody has yet. Every outright motorcycle land speed record since 1956 has been set in Utah. Obviously, it would be good if it was longer, because it would be less important to accelerate smoothly up to top speed and you wouldn't have to worry too much about losing traction as you got up to it. If you had longer to accelerate you'd also need less power, so there'd be less strain on the machine, but it's a vicious circle. If people had a longer track, they'd still use more power and aim to go 450, not 400. We always want more power.

A year to the week after the Ulster crash I was on a flight from London to Salt Lake City, Utah, with my big sister Sally, some folk from Triumph's Leicestershire headquarters and the regular North One TV lot for a week of testing in the streamliner.

After a two-hour drive from the airport, we reached the hotel in Wendover, the nearest town to the salt flats, late on Wednesday. The streamliner wasn't due to arrive from Portland until the next day, but I'd been told that another team aiming to break the motorcycle land speed record was testing on the salt, and I was dead keen to have a mooch around. I wanted to find out as much as I could about the job, so early the next morning we drove out mob-handed to see what was occurring. Looking at how another team and rider were set up was an opportunity too good to miss.

Ten miles from Wendover, off Interstate 80, there's a turn-off that leads to the salt flats. The tarmac ends, and there are two signs telling you, if you needed telling, that you're on Bonneville Salt Flats. The salt stretches as far as the eye can see, to mountains over 20 miles away. The land is public, so people can drive on to it, but there are traffic cones set out and folk parked to discourage people from driving out when racers are testing.

Four or five miles on to the salt we found the BUB team and its owner, Denis Manning. Manning has been involved with motorcycle record breakers since 1970, when the Harley-Davidson streamliner he had summat to do with set a record speed of 254.84 mph with the late American road racer Cal Rayborn in control. Manning used to own a company making motorcycle exhausts called BUB, and his bike, the BUB Seven Streamliner, was the world's fastest motorcycle in 2006 and 2009.

I looked into a bit of history of motorcycle speed attempts. The official motorbike record broke the 300 mph barrier in 1975, when Don Vesco went 302.9, in

Silver Bird, a twin-engined streamliner using Yamaha TZ700 two-stroke road-racing engines. Vesco broke his own record in 1978, with *Lightning Bolt*, a new streamliner with two turbocharged Kawasaki Z1000 engines, going 318.6. That record stood for 12 years until Dave Campos, in a twin-engined Harley-Davidson, went 322.2 mph. It was another 16 years before Rocky Robinson in the turbocharged twin Suzuki Hayabusa-powered Ack Attack went quicker, raising the speed by 20 mph. Just two days later Chris Carr in the BUB broke it again, and became the first man to do an average of over 350 mph in a motorcycle streamliner. Over the next four years the record went back and forth between the BUB and Ack Attack, with Rocky Robinson and the Ack Attack coming out on top in September 2010, with their 376 mph two-way average, but their top recorded speed was 394 mph.

Setting a land speed record is not just a case of hitting the fastest ever speed for a second. The machine must do two passes through a timed mile, one in each direction to account for tailwinds or gradients. And the second run must start within two hours of the first one. A one-way speed is determined as the average speed through the mile, and bikes are often going faster at the end of the timed mile than when starting it. The two speeds are added together and divided by two to give the record speed.

The BUB team were dead friendly. Manning and his son worked together with a crew of six or seven trusted old hands. It was obvious they'd been at it for years, and they were happy for me to ask questions, though I'd been warned to take everything Manning told me with a pinch of salt (there was no shortage of that). I'm not stupid, though. I know enough to realise when someone's bullshitting, and I didn't think they were. Or not too much, anyway.

Manning explained that their bike had been in development for 16 years and had a purpose-built V4 engine in it. They cast the casings, the full lot. I was impressed. It got me half-thinking that just bolting two motorbike engines in a streamliner was taking the easy route, but other than the BUB bike, every record since 1966 has been held by a streamliner powered by two modified production-bike engines. The bike that currently holds the record, Ack Attack, has two Suzuki Hayabusa engines in it.

The other thing about the BUB is that it is the only streamliner, except for the Triumph, that has a monocoque chassis. By that, I mean the body of the machine is what gives it its strength. All the other streamliners have a steel frame or skeleton that the bodywork is bolted to. Manning and Markstaller agree that the monocoque is the safest construction, but one of the main organisations that run speed trials on Bonneville, the Southern

California Timing Association, don't allow monocoque bikes to run at their meetings. They're more set up for cars than bikes, so Manning started his own BUB Speed Trials, purely for motorcycles, and the meeting still runs now, but with his ex-daughter-in-law running it. The reason fans of monocoque designs are convinced they're better than regular space frames with bodywork attached is because they believe a monocoque keeps its shape better in a violent crash and stays sliding on its side, while a space frame streamliner can lose bodywork more easily in an impact and develop a sharp edge that can dig into salt and flip it into the air.

The week before I left for Utah, another racer aiming to break the land speed record had died testing at Bonneville. Sam Wheeler was 72, and he had been racing on the salt flats since 1963. He'd gone over 200 mph as early as 1970, and his top speed was 355 mph. He built his own streamliners, and the current one was powered by a single Suzuki Hayabusa Turbo.

I'd read that, in 2006, he'd crashed at over 350 mph and survived. This time eyewitnesses reckoned Wheeler was doing closer to 200 mph when the 500bhp streamliner started fishtailing. I was told it slid for a while, which is the best you can hope for when a streamliner crashes, but then flew up in the air and came down hard, and then it did the same again. The rider was alive when he left Bonneville, but died soon after. The news was horrible, but it had also got me even more interested. Before I heard this I'd thought breaking a land speed record was just a case of pointing the right machine at the horizon and getting on the throttle. I didn't think it was much of a challenge for the rider, but now I knew that it was this dangerous, it was a different kettle of fish.

The BUB team had a new rider too. Both of BUB's speed records had been set by Chris Carr, the dirt-track legend and multiple champion. Now they had Valerie Thompson, a 49-year-old drag racer and Bonneville regular, from Las Vegas. Lovely woman, and, like all the BUB team, dead friendly and open. This four- or five-day test was her first time getting to grips with the streamliner, and she'd spent the time being towed behind a truck at 50 mph to get used to balancing the bike. These streamliners are heavy, and you're strapped into a seat so you don't have the same influence over the balance of the bike – you can't just put your foot down to stop yourself falling over. Valerie has been 217 mph on a BMW S1000RR superbike, so she wasn't a messer, but the streamliner was something else. She had it on its side a couple of times during her test, but no one was batting an eyelid. They seemed to expect a couple of gentle crashes.

The BUB lot were switched-on blokes. Their streamliner looked a bit Heath Robinson, but bloody impressive to say it was only a shed effort. In the 16 years they'd been working on it, BUB and their sponsors had obviously spent some money, but now it looked a bit rough around the edges. It has done impressive speeds, having gone over 140 mph faster than the Triumph streamliner had up to that point. Talking to them while we were waiting for the Triumph to turn up put me on the back foot a bit. No one was slagging Matt Markstaller off, but the 16 years of development and one-off engine stuck in my mind.

During that first morning on the salt flats I also met Mike Cook, who felt like the father of Bonneville. If you want to do any private testing or book the track to attempt a record, you see him. He's a car racer whose dad was a drag racer, and his son is a drag racer and Bonneville racer, too. He's in his sixties, and small and weathered from day after day of being out in the baking sun. He knew everyone, had driven his own Ford Thunderbird at over 300 mph, and he had recently restored a car called *Goldenrod*, which was the world's fastest wheel-driven, piston-powered car, just as the era of turbine and jet cars started raising the speeds and claiming the outright land speed records. In 1965, *Goldenrod* took the record from Donald Campbell's *Bluebird*, so to be trusted with restoring that car proves how respected he is. I talked to Mike Cook on and off all week. He put my mind at ease over a load of stuff. We had a good few yarns, both out on the salt and in a cool little bar called Carmen's Black and White. He was dead friendly, just a brilliant bloke. His crew of helpers drive up and down in trucks, pulling heavy graders made from steel beams welded together to smooth the salt as best they can, and he put Triumph in touch with everyone from the fire and ambulance folk to the official timers that we'd need to run out there.

The BUB lot liked to talk, and I was happy to listen. I got the feeling they'd told the stories a hundred times before, but it was all new to me. Denis Manning, who named the bike after his company, BUB – Big Ugly Bastard – told me he got the shape of his bike after watching salmon swim up a river, and it sounded like a good story. When Matt Markstaller arrived later in the day he'd also heard the same salmon yarn, but he pulled a face that gave me the impression he didn't believe it. Where BUB were clever engineers and good old boys, Matt was different. When it came to deciding the shape for his streamliner he researched the most aerodynamic shapes American engineers had ever come up with. The shape he chose in the end was a plane fuselage designed by NACA, the National Advisory Committee for Aeronautics, the forerunner to NASA. He wasn't guessing or spinning a yarn about fish – he was dealing with scientifically proven hard facts.

Markstaller brought a big team of helpers to keep the streamliner fettled, but there were a few main men. Most important was Matt himself, who designed and oversaw the building of the machine. Also there was Ed from Carpenter Racing, in New Jersey, who built the engines. This was the first time I'd met Ed, and I hit it off with him straight away. We were both into Snap-on tools, and I could tell from the way he wields a spanner that he knows what he's on about. He has a certain way of building engines, and we spoke for hours about compression ratios, intake ports and lock-up clutches.

James was the brilliant electronics man. You'd think he'd come out of MIT or something, and maybe he has. A very clever man who would answer my questions about the rate of acceleration and the length of track by telling me I needed to accelerate at 0.2 g to reach 400 mph in five miles, but to achieve that we had to have an aerodynamic drag coefficient of friction of 0.1 – or summat like that. He's not playing at it.

The other main man was Dave – Crazy Dave. He was in his seventies, the oldest man on the team, and was an experienced drag racer, expert welder and machinist with long white hair and an eye patch who had machined and welded a load of stuff for Matt. I looked at some of the stuff he'd made on old-fashioned, manual milling machines and couldn't work out how he'd done it without the help of a modern CNC machine.

The other team members were friends or Markstaller family members, and had jobs from checking the coolant levels in the belly tanks to filling the fuel tank, removing the panels to get to the engine, cleaning the screen, checking tyre pressures and tyre condition before every run, driving the tow truck … There were about 50 items to check before every run. Ed would only get his hands on it if something wasn't going quite right. He'd done all his hard work back in New Jersey, when he'd tuned and built the engines.

The Triumph lot had allowed BUB to continue using the track for an extra day after they'd lost one because of rain. It was no skin off our nose, because our bike wasn't arriving until midday Thursday at the earliest. In the end, it didn't arrive till gone three in the afternoon.

I was itching to get out in it as soon as I could, and Matt said I could have my first go at getting to grips with it that day. The streamliner had been transported in a trailer and was suspended under a heavy steel cradle, which held it about 3 feet off the floor so it was easier to work on. The team checked everything over, then, late that afternoon, I got the nod to get in my kit, ready for the first ride.

I would be towed behind a big American GMC Yukon, so the streamliner was fitted with big stabilisers, bolted on halfway down its length, to do the same job as those on a kid's first bike. They'd be left on until I proved I had the hang of keeping it upright. The Triumph also had little retractable alloy legs, less than a foot long, that popped in and out of the bike's belly when I pressed a button. When the stabilisers were eventually taken off, these would keep the bike from falling over when I came to a stop.

I climbed into the bike's cockpit, and it was snug. I'd lost weight since I first tested it, and that helped, but there was still a knack of getting in and out, because it was so bloody tight. To get in, I first had to brush all the salt off the sole of my right shoe, stand in the bike, then brush the other off. When I was standing in the gap in front of the seat, I lowered myself down and slid one leg, then the other, under the dashboard, pushed my backside into the back of the seat and tucked my head under the carbon-fibre loop that was designed to protect me if it ever started barrel-rolling. The bike was fitted with five-point harnesses. Wide, heavy-duty seat straps went over each shoulder, and two around the waist, and they all met at one buckle over my belly. I also had wrist straps that fastened to the harness, so if I crashed my arms would stay in the cockpit instead of flailing outside and getting crushed by the rolling bike, which weighs close to a ton.

I wore my regular AGV helmet for the early practice runs, even though it wasn't approved for record attempts. I wanted to wear something I was comfy in and wouldn't distract me, because everything else was so unfamiliar. The team said they'd leave the canopy lid off for the first towing runs. I wasn't going to be moving quick enough to need it, and it was a bit easier to talk and make myself understood without it. The canopy was a curved screen in a carbon-fibre frame with a trick release mechanism. It looked like it was straight off a jet fighter. It wasn't hinged like a door or a hatch – it had to be lifted into place and clipped down. If I ever needed to get out in a hurry, I'd just release the catch and push it off. A long climbing rope was tied to the stabiliser legs and attached to the back of the Yukon. The car set off very gently and slowly. I had my hands on the controls and was getting the feel for how much input I had to give to steer this nearly 26-foot-long bike. Our pits were set up at the one-mile mark, with the course being seven miles of usable salt, 120 feet wide, and we headed east down the track.

By the time we'd got a few miles under our wheels I had the thing balanced at 35 mph. Matt was in the back of the 4x4, with its hatchback open, and Nat the cameraman was set up next to him. Matt must have been surprised I'd got the hang of it so quickly, because he was saying, 'Well, will you look at that?'

I'd heard that Jason DiSalvo, the Triumph team's only previous rider, took a week to get up off the stabilisers and balancing while being towed, so I didn't know how hard it was going to be. But I was up and balancing on the very first run. I had to give constant little adjustments to the steering, but I got the hang of it, and I'm no Danny MacAskill, so I don't know why anyone else would have so much bother.

Even though Triumph had allowed the BUB team to keep practising on the salt for free, and were dead friendly earlier in the day, someone had squealed to Mike Cook about us doing this little 50 mph towing run without the ambulance being on the track. Perhaps they were trying to play mind games early on. It seemed a bit daft.

The original plan was that we'd be out on the salt at 6.30am and off by midday, because the wind was usually calmest early in the morning. There are rules that don't allow streamliners to run with side wind of more than 4 mph, so there can be a lot of sitting around waiting for the weather. Mike Cook also explained that the desert sun brings moisture to the surface of the salt as the day goes on, so it's the opposite of what you'd expect. You'd think the track would be damp overnight and dry out during the day, but it doesn't. It was all new to me, and I just wanted to be out there every minute we could.

I'd get up at five and walk over the road to the petrol station to have coffee and porridge, because it was cheaper than the hotel. I'd meet the TV lot in the car park at quarter-past six and drive out to the salt in their rented Transit van. Triumph had brought three camper vans, one for Triumph and their photographers to work out of, one for the TV lot and one for me and Matt to use, but I didn't like the idea of having one. I don't want to be treated differently to the rest of the team. I try to explain to them that I'm only a wanker, nowt special, and I don't want or need special treatment. There was a medical helicopter booked while we were running. It was there from seven in the morning, and the crew ended up hanging around in the motorhome that had been brought for me, so it wasn't going to waste. I will admit it was good for having a wee in without having to drive to the Honey Buckets, the portable toilets at mile zero. We made the rule to drive down to those for a number two, and we also knew that if someone drove off in a car on their own, they were going on a Honey Bucket run.

Day two, Friday, the first proper day, started with more tow runs. We'd leave the pit, at mile one, and head to the seven-mile marker, then turn around and come back. Everyone was dead pleased with the progress. We hadn't been over 60 mph, but people kept saying it had taken DiSalvo more than a week to get to this stage. By early afternoon we moved on to braking practice. People reckon the braking part is the most dangerous part of a record run, but this was just slow-speed stuff. We did over 20 practices, being towed up to speed then braking down to a standstill. The brake was a carbon-carbon set-up, which means carbon-fibre brake pads on a carbon-fibre disc. It can deal with a lot more heat than a conventional steel or iron disc, and the hotter it gets the more it grips. This type is used in F1 and MotoGP, but Matt got the streamliner's brakes from the company that made the brakes for the space shuttle. All the practices boiled the brake fluid and the brakes eventually faded, nearly making me crash into the back of the tow car. It wouldn't be a problem if I ever had to brake from more than 400 mph, because there would be more air passing around it – and I'll also have parachutes to do a lot of the braking.

The waiting around meant I could spend more time looking at the bike and quizzing the people who built it. I'd seen the streamliner before, and knew how well made it was. No expense was spared. It looked just the same as when I'd seen it last time, all nice bits and bobs, any bare metal anodised, and it was well beyond anything someone would build in their shed. The front end had hub-centre steering, like a Bimota Tesi or Vyrus, not regular forks. Matt chose this design to keep the front end lower. The front wheel bearings were $8,000 each, and there were two of them. Matt ordered them from Germany. The special grease for the bearings was $200, not £10 from Cromwell's. Even Matt said he wouldn't normally go to these lengths, but Triumph wanted the best.

I found out a lot more about the engines. They were modified Triumph Rocket III motors. They're the biggest production motorcycle engine, at 2294 cc, but while land speed record bikes can have more than one engine, the maximum cylinder capacity is 3000 cc, so two standard

Rocket III engines would be too big. When I wrote *When You Dead, You Dead* I got a couple of details about the engine wrong. I thought Carpenter Racing had reduced the size of the bore to reduce capacity, but they'd kept the stock piston size and reduced the stroke with a new crank to get each engine's cylinder capacity down to 1480 cc. The crank had titanium conrods fitted and low compression pistons. Carpenter had designed a new cam too, but the valves were standard.

Both engines were fitted with their own turbos, but they were nothing fancy and had internal wastegates. The engine was fed by bigger flow fuel injectors. There wasn't room for an intercooler, but the bike would run on methanol, not petrol, and that runs cooler.

There were still a lot of original Triumph parts left. The crank cases, gearbox and most of the clutch were all standard, but Carpenter had made a centrifugal pressure plate for the clutch that made it like an automatic. There was no clutch lever or pedal.

At the end of day two, half-three on a Friday afternoon, the weather looked good enough for my first power run, but there was a problem with a wheel speed sensor, which was affecting the traction control. I didn't think it would matter for this first slow run, but then Nik Ellwood from Triumph said the helicopter was only booked till four, so there was no point in rushing and running without the sensor. I wanted to get the run in and told him I'd sign anything to say I knew the risks and was happy to run without the helicopter, but contracts had been organised between Spellman and Triumph, and Nik wouldn't let me. When people started talking about contracts I felt I had to explain to the team that I wasn't being paid by Triumph or any of their sponsors to be there.

Nik was the one who'd suggested I should be the man to ride the thing, so I was dead grateful for that. He had a tough job, being the middle man between the team, the factory, sponsors, journalists, photographers and me. I wouldn't want to do it.

The next morning, I was towed up to the seven-mile point for the first test run. Following me was Matt and his eldest son, Ian, in a rental Camaro muscle car; the film crew come in a 4x4, Mike Cook in his massive pick-up truck, Eric the Öhlins suspension man in his car, plus Ed and James the electronics man in another rental car.

The streamliner had a massive turning circle, and we'd made the mistake on the very first towing run of going off the track to turn it around behind the 4x4, and it had got totally caked in the softer salt where it hadn't been graded by Mike Cook's track workers. The front wheel was now pushed on to a metal skid with a long rope attached to it, and six people pulled and pushed the bike around 180 degrees, to point back to where I'd come from, while I had my foot on the brake.

This was it, the first run. I was told to go no more than

80 mph, and I had the stabilisers fitted. Now that I was more used to things the canopy was fastened down, like it would be for every future run, and I got ready to start the engines. The starting procedure is this: Matt holds one finger up and I start engine number one, then he gives me the thumbs up before putting up two fingers, for me to start engine number two. With both engines running and everything looking and sounding good, he puts his thumb up and walks away to his car. I have to leave it ten seconds before I set off.

The bike is already in gear when I start the engines, and it has that automatic clutch, so I just twist the throttle. I went 50 feet, if that, before the bike lost drive. The cars that were following me all stopped and people ran out to come and take the canopy off. I explained that it just lost power, and the crew set about taking off the long engine cover panels to see what had happened. They worked out that there was no drive from the engine to the back wheel. There were a lot of things that could have been causing it. The drive train of the Triumph streamliner was a trick set-up. The two Triumph Rocket III motors drive through their standard five-speed gearboxes, but the two gearboxes are linked with a shaft that drives another short shaft through a Porsche CV joint. The output from there acts like a shaft drive on a regular Triumph Rocket III leading to a rear hub. Instead of the Triumph hub, the streamliner has a bevel gear set-up from a racing speedboat. Matt didn't know what was broken – all we knew was that there was no drive between the engines and the rear wheel. We didn't want to risk towing the bike the six miles back to the pits in case something came loose, started flailing around and damaged another part of the bike, so we had to wait while the 4x4 drove back, bolted the towing bracket to the frame that picks the bike off the floor, brought it up to the bike, raised the bike then towed it back to mile one.

It was heading towards Saturday dinnertime, and different causes were being guessed at. There was talk of best-case scenarios. Some problems could be fixed relatively easily, others might bugger us up for days. At the very best, we'd lost the day. There were only three to go, and who knew what the weather was going to do?

A good hour after getting back to the pits, we found out that the driveshaft had snapped, where a spline has been welded to a shortened shaft. Crazy Dave knew someone in Salt Lake City, 120 miles away, who could weld it. We – me, Matt and Dave – got in the rental Charger and set off. Dave's mate was a bloody brilliant welder. He told Matt that the shaft wasn't the steel he was told it was.

It was early evening when we got back to Wendover and I walked down to Carmen's Black and White Bar, the place I'd been told about. It's a wooden building, definitely nothing fancy. It looks like a big shed that's been painted white and it has no windows. You'd never find it if you weren't looking for it, as it's down a backstreet with mobile homes parked around it. It doesn't look promising, but you walk in and see the walls covered with posters and photos of Bonneville racers. It's run by Carmen, a women in her sixties, who is the only person who works there. Sally was there with *Sideburn* editor Gary Inman, who'd also travelled out to see what was going on. I had a bottle of beer as I looked at the photos, then Mike Cook came in. Carmen made me a cup of tea and I talked to Mike for an hour. He'd never raced a bike, but I could ask him loads of questions about the salt and how machines behaved out on it. He told me that if I ran off the track I didn't have to panic, I just had to steer back on. I walked back to the hotel with Sal and Gary. Sal wanted something to eat so we stopped at the Subway, next to the petrol station where I had breakfast, but I still couldn't bring myself to eat there after having so many on the Tour Divide.

The next morning we were out at the pits at 6.30 as usual. The bike was nearly back together, and I thought we'd be ready to go as soon as the helicopter landed, but we hardly ever were. If Mark McCarville, the foreman from the TAS team, were here the team would work as long as it took after we finished riding to be ready to go the next morning, but this lot seemed to leave a load of jobs for the next morning. I couldn't understand it, but I kept my nose out. I'm sure there was a good reason.

I wasn't being impatient, but I had a lot to learn about the land speed job, and the best way to learn is by riding the thing – seat time, as the Americans put it. Before too long everything was bolted together and ready to tow up again. I didn't have any shoes on, because room was so tight in the nose that I was having a bit of a struggle to comfortably get my foot on the brake pedal. I wanted to ride in just my socks, but Matt made me wear driving boots.

At the far end of the track the stabilisers were bolted back on. They were adjusted so the stabilisers' wheels were off the floor, like they were on the towing runs. They were there just to catch me if I tipped over. First gear needed to be engaged by hand, so the side panel was removed, then fitted back in place with about 20 screws. I started the engines, got the thumbs up and set off.

Like anything on two wheels, the streamliner is at its least stable at slow speeds, so I'm on the little wheels of the retractable landing gear legs till I get up to 30 mph, then I'm balanced.

Unsurprisingly, the controls are different to a regular bike. I have two handles or joysticks, I suppose, bolted to either side of the cockpit, next to my thighs. They're aeroplane grips and just move forwards and backwards, not side to side. I twist the throttle, as normal, but it's vertical, not horizontal. The brake is operated by a foot pedal – there is no hand lever. On the grips I have two buttons to change gear, one each for up and down. I have two more buttons, up and down for landing gear.

I have a MoTeC dash, with loads of information on it, but I'm only looking at speed. If anything happens to oil pressure, oil temperature or water temperature, it'll flash warning lights at me, so I don't have to be reading the numbers.

I accelerated steadily away, short shifting before the turbo boost came in. Behind me, out of my line of sight, all the cars were following. I had a radio earpiece and I could just about hear, and talk to, Matt.

From mile seven to mile five and a half the streamliner's wheels were following ruts, like a car follows truck's ruts on a worn-out motorway, but I could control it. I also had double-vision when the canopy was fitted. I was seeing two of every mile marker, so I closed one eye.

The Triumph felt like Nige – pulling on the lead so hard it's strangling itself, as all it wants to do is run faster. The first run went without a bother. It was so easy it was a bit boring. I felt confident to go faster, but I was there to jump through all the hoops that the Bonneville authorities put in front of me, and I had to prove I could safely handle the bike at certain speeds before moving to the next speed, so I kept it close to 80. I was doing 3,200 rpm in third gear.

James, the electronics man, confirmed that I actually touched 92 mph, and I wanted to go again, but the streamliner needed checking. The side panels were taken off and the belly tanks where the radiators were mounted in tanks of water were removed to have their temperatures checked.

Mike Cook, who followed behind on every run I did in the practice week, told the team that he'd never seen anyone get to grips with balancing as quickly as I did, but 90 mph is not 400 mph, so I wasn't getting too excited. Then the wind got up. Mike won't let any record bikes run on his track in more than a 4 mph crosswind, and this was all of 10 mph, so the rest of the day was a write-off. We were making progress, but I just wanted to keep riding the thing. I did a bit of filming with the TV lot then got back to the hotel to work on this book.

I was in the pits raring to go at 6.30 on Monday morning. We only had two more days of testing and I hadn't even been over 100 mph yet. I'd been faster than that pedalling a pushbike along a Welsh beach. Then, when I thought we were finally going to do the run, I was told I would have to practise getting in and out of the cockpit, so I knew what to do in an emergency. Why didn't we practise this the day before when the wind was too high to do anything else?

I did need the practice emergency exit, though. My first attempt wasn't very good – I was rushing and got my legs stuck. It made me remember that I had to get out from under the dashboard one leg at a time. Everyone was happy with my next attempt, so the bike, still suspended above the salt in its frame, could be pushed on to the track, lowered, tied to the truck and pulled to mile seven.

This was supposed to be my 120 mph run, but Matt said I could take it to 150 and no one would complain. This would be my second power run, and the first without the stabilisers. I started the engines, moved 20 feet and the engines stalled. Everyone ran out to the bike and took the panels off while I stayed in the cockpit, helmet on, canopy off. It wasn't a quick fix so I eventually climbed out. One motor started but the other sounded like it had a flat battery. James and Ed thought it might be mechanical. I didn't think it was, because it petered out like it had run out of petrol. When the laptop was plugged in it told us that a cam sensor wasn't reading, but we didn't know if that was because something had broken and damaged it, or not.

We towed the bike back to base and the team started investigating. I wasn't getting frustrated – I just wondered what it was. It turned out just to be a cam sensor problem, and in an hour the bike was running properly, with the same sensor. I was surprised they didn't swap it while they had the chance, but the bike seemed to be running alright. Luckily, the weather hadn't changed for the worse, so we headed back to mile seven. From there it was impossible to see the pits, and if anyone needed anything it was a 12-mile round trip to fetch it.

This time everything went according to plan. I was riding with one eye, because of the double vision. I had been swapping eyes during the practice towing runs, but it took too long for the other eye to focus, so I just kept one closed.

When I set off it felt like the wind got me and I couldn't get it balanced, so I left the landing gear legs down longer than normal till I got it right. Mark started shouting down the radio, but I couldn't hear what he was saying, so I stopped. He was telling me the legs weren't up, but I knew that. Just leave me to it.

After going through the starting procedure again I set off, and this time I got settled quickly. I looked at the speedo expecting to see 60 and I was already doing 120 mph, the maximum I was supposed to do, but Matt had already said I could do 150. Next thing I knew I was doing 180, 190 – it came so easy – so I thought, Let's see what it'll do. There was no sensation of speed, which was why it could feel boring. The team had set a rev limit, electronically, which stopped me revving the bike as hard as I wanted. This was the first time I tested the parachutes. I released them in the order Matt told me: right hand release first, then left. This deploys the big one first.

The convoy of cars caught up. James plugged in the laptop and confirmed the speed, 219 mph. It felt like we were getting somewhere now. We weren't doing two-way runs or speeds over a timed mile yet, just recording peak speeds, and at 219 I felt I could have had one hand off the controls, smoking a cigarette. Everyone was keen to get the bike ready for another run, and everything was checked within an hour.

It wasn't long before I was towed out to the seven-mile marker again, and the rev limit had been increased a bit. Again, everything went smoothly with the start-up procedure and launching off, but it didn't stay that way for long. At close to 200 mph the bike got out of shape, and the whole thing was fishtailing. It was moving so much I was nearly looking out the side of window. I thought it was going on its side. I was in a hell of a wobble, but the more I fought it, the calmer it got. It's the opposite on a TT bike – if you hang too tightly on to one of them when it's tankslapping, it sends the movement to you, and it gets worse and chucks you off. In the streamliner I locked my knees under my arms, which calmed it down, and it came in line again. I lost about 10 mph while I was fighting it, then I gathered my thoughts and got back on the throttle to reach 256 mph. I had now gone faster than Jason DiSalvo had gone in the Triumph.

I was on the throttle non-stop for 20 seconds, but the

engine was still hitting a limiter and not letting me go any faster. I rolled the throttle at mile three because I was bored of sitting at 256. Mike Cook had turned the big mile-marker numbers that line either side of the track around so I knew where I was. It's deceiving how far the pit camp is away. I got to the two-mile marker, so one mile from the pits, before pulling the parachute. By now I'd been told to use the small one first, the opposite of what I was told at first. Then I got everything settled, going down a couple of gears, giving it a bit of brake, and then at 40 mph I pressed the button to get the landing-gear legs down.

The TV lot's on-board cameras had caught the action, and you could see the horizon tipping from side to side as the streamliner fishtailed. The team looked at it and Matt didn't know what was causing it, but I could see his gears turning as I was talking to him. He was coming up with different ideas, and I liked the way he was thinking.

He reckoned it could be the rear tyre. It had quite a square shape and he thought I might have rolled off the edge of it, and that put it in a weave. He asked the team to fit a bigger tail fin to help stability and called it a day.

The wobble didn't make me want to stop riding it, but I planned to wear the OMP helmet with the HANS device now. HANS stands for Head and Neck Support. The helmet is tethered to a shoulder harness that limits how much the head can move forward or back in relation to the body, and should stop injuries from whiplash movements. A lot of car-racing series, including F1, have made them compulsory, and I was used to riding the thing by now, so I didn't need the familiarity of the AGV any more. I wanted the added safety of a helmet with a HANS device, and bike helmets don't have the screw holes to fit one to.

I headed back to the hotel to keep working on the book. I began to wonder how many boys had been killed doing the land speed job and, for the first time in my life, started seriously thinking about writing a will. If it does go on its side at 250 mph, what's it going to do? It's going to get messy. Matt said that the streamliner's body had been built to withstand 50 g, but I haven't. I wasn't the only one who thought it might be dangerous. I heard that the insurance policy to cover me for the attempt cost over £60,000.

When it got wild, I realised how fast it was going. For each go on the flats, I was towed away from the pits and then I made the run back towards them, but after the wobble I got uncomfortable with the thought of heading back towards the pits. If I lost control, who was I going to plough into? I'd rather head towards Floating Mountain, in the east, so if I lost control I wouldn't crash into anything. Matt wanted me to keep doing it how we had all week, running from the Floating Mountain end of the course, because he reckoned the salt was soft between miles one and two and it would affect acceleration. I couldn't tell the difference between hard and soft salt when I was in the thing, but it tried to follow ruts, and if it did I had to go with it.

Tuesday started the same way as usual: cheap porridge in the Shell station and ten minutes' drive out to the salt. The helicopter landed 100 metres from the pits at seven, while the team were doing their morning pre-ride checks. It was 9 August, and the last day of testing. We didn't know if the taller tailfin was going to make any difference to stability, but there was only one way to find out.

The mood was different. Everything was a bit quieter after the previous day's wobble. When I climbed into the cockpit to be towed out, Sal came up to me and said, 'Go steady.' I laughed and reminded her that I wasn't here to go steady.

They towed me out to just beyond the seven-mile marker this time. It always felt bumpy and rough as hell when I was being towed out, but the faster the streamliner went, the smoother it became. The front end has three fancy, Superbike-spec Öhlins TTX shocks to damp it, and they seemed to work better at speed.

This was the 250 mph run, but, as usual, I wanted to go faster. The run was smoother than the previous day's. The streamliner was still following ruts, but I could deal with it. I was always tweaking the steering, using the horizon as the guide, keeping that dead level.

The machine wasn't talking to me – I wasn't getting any feedback. It was all visual. I changed gear when the light came on, and the traction control was looking after itself. It sounds easy, but it isn't. Nothing went wrong, but it didn't reach the speeds I wanted it to.

I pulled the parachute at two miles and coasted to a stop a couple of hundred metres from the pits. The recorded speed was 274.2 mph. Matt seemed pleased enough, and there were no big wobbles this time. Triumph were happy because it meant the new streamliner was their fastest ever, and had something to tell people. The top-speed record we broke was set in 1966, by Bob Leppan in Gyronaut X-1, with two air-cooled, bored-out 650 Meriden twins, so if we couldn't go faster than that, with 50 years of technological advances, two turbos and twice the cylinder capacity behind us, there was something badly wrong. That's why, for me at least, it was just a step to where we wanted to be and not much more. We want to break Ack Attack's world land speed record, and that stands at a two-way average of 376.363 mph, over 100 mph faster than the Triumph streamliner has ever been. The team, and Triumph, want to be the first bike over 400 mph. I was happy enough. We'd moved in the right direction all week, and once we went over 230 mph it was all into the unknown for the team.

I did want another run, to try to go over 300 mph, but Nik from Triumph wasn't keen and Matt agreed, explaining that there wasn't a lot of point putting more miles on the streamliner because we wouldn't learn much from going just 26 mph faster. The first thing I have to do at the record meeting, whenever that will be, is to do a 300 mph run in front of the FIM, the Fédération Internationale de Motocyclisme, to prove I can do it, but it would've been good for my own peace of mind to know I had done over 300 mph before we packed it in. Having said that, it was trick being out there, being involved with something with this much planning and effort behind it. I am honoured that Triumph chose me, but it's not going to be plain sailing. Mark is concerned about the state of the salt. He made it clear that everything has to be perfect to have any chance of breaking the record. He explained that if I get wheelspin during acceleration on a record run I should just park it, wait for the tow truck, go back to the beginning and try again. If it's not a perfect run, don't bother burning fuel.

We had a team meeting before we left. Matt said he was going to look for newer tyres, to see if that was the cause of the fishtailing. The data showed that the engines need more fuel to make the power for a record run, but the standard coils that were fitted weren't man enough to deliver a spark that could ignite the additional fuel, so they have to fit different coils. We said our goodbyes, not knowing when we'd be back. Matt was going to travel back to Bonneville within the week to see if he thought the salt would be good enough for the attempt that was planned for late August, but he didn't seem hopeful.

With that one and only run on Tuesday, we were all done before nine in the morning on the last day, so the TV lot had me visit Wendover's little library to do some bits for the programme, before I went back to the hotel to do some more work on the book. I was flying home the next day, but I still had one more thing to do on Bonneville Salt Flats first.

CHAPTER 19

Clinging on for grim death, sawing at the steering wheel to keep it in a straight line

AFTER ANOTHER NIGHT in Wendover's Montego Bay hotel I walked over the road to have porridge in the petrol station, before heading out to the salt flats for the last time on this week-long trip. The Triumph lot had packed up the day before and headed off to jet-wash the crusted salt that was blathered all over their hire cars and camper vans, hoping to avoid getting stung with the $1,000 fines the hire companies had hidden in their small print. Everyone was happy enough with how things had gone, but more work had to be done on the streamliner.

One trick six-cylinder, 3-litre machine had gone, to be replaced by another trick six-cylinder, 3.5-litre machine. The black Transit, FT13 AFK, had been stored at Radical Ventures' garage, on the outskirts of Las Vegas, since May's Nevada Open Road Challenge race. The TV lot had the idea of killing two birds with one stone. They and James from Radical in Peterborough looked at the record for the world's fastest van, and reckoned my Transit could break it.

All the word, when we were at the Nevada race, was about the Transit getting to 170 mph and feeling like it wanted to keep going when I had to back off. It did feel to me that it had a bit more in it, but only enough for about 180 mph, and only if it had a long enough stretch of road to keep going. Ewan, the TV director who'd been on that job, had an inkling it could do 200 mph at Bonneville, but I never thought it could. I was the least confident, and I knew the salt would add drag that the engine would have to overcome, but I didn't know how much.

James had flown over from Radical's Peterborough headquarters and met with Brian from the Las Vegas outfit. James was there to handle all the computer side of things, mapping the fuel and the engine management, making any changes to squeeze more power out of the engine. The Transit had been brought up in a big enclosed trailer, pulled by a V8 pick-up. The van, my van, looked mint, with just a bit of shop dust on it, and it was good to see it again. Even though loads had changed in the interior, it still felt like my van.

Compared to the streamliner there was hardly any preparation or messing about to do before a run – just get in and turn on the Transit. Brian parked the truck and trailer at mile zero, an easy walk to the Honey Buckets. Mike Cook was there again, like he had been all week.

Brian and James got on with unloading the Transit, then Paul from North One, who had been nicknamed the President because he looked like Bill Clinton, rigged up the interior with miniature cameras to film the onboard footage. While he was on with that, the medical helicopter from Salt Lake City landed, letting us know that it was seven o'clock and we could run as soon as we were ready.

The record we were aiming for was 177 mph, set by Supervan 2, the two-thirds-size Ford promotional van that was fitted with a Cosworth DFV V8 Formula One/Le Mans 24-hour engine. This was just a peak speed, not a two-way or an average through a timed mile. All that had been changed since the Nevada Open Road Challenge race was a new set of Pirelli P Zero supercar tyres.

I was in my race overalls. I got in it and was told to just go 100 mph to get a feel for it, then stop at the two-mile marker so Brian could test the tyre temperatures, but I either didn't hear them or I forgot, because I thought I'd see what it could do on the return run. I checked that all the numbers were right – I could see oil temperature, water temperature and boost temperature gauges – and they were all good, so I thought I might as well give it the berries.

When the salt was a bit rutty I was clinging on for grim death, sawing at the steering wheel to keep it in a straight line, but as soon as I got it on the smooth stuff it was spot on.

On the return run the van did 155 mph, but I had my foot to the board for what must have been a minute and it wouldn't go over that speed. I got back to the truck and James plugged in the laptop, had a look at the data and increased the turbo boost.

Turbos increase an engine's power by forcing more air and fuel, the charge, into the combustion chamber to be burnt. It does this by compressing the air. More air and fuel equals a bigger bang and, in turn, more power. Increasing the boost means compressing the air more to force a greater amount of mixture into the combustion chamber, to increase power. You can't just keep increasing boost, though. More heat is generated, and the increase in power puts a strain on the engine that will eventually lead to something failing.

Conditions were perfect, but the van felt a bit weavy, so it was a good time to swap the AGV for the car helmet and HANS device. Mike Cook reminded me that I had to wear a wrist strap as well, but I couldn't find mine. I probably left it on the seat of the streamliner. James and Brian had a dig about in the back of their trailer and found one I could use. I only needed it on the right arm, the one closest to the side window.

I put the diff lock on to try to stop the van's back end squirrelling. This locks the rear differential so both wheels spin at the same rate. Normally, rear-wheel-drive cars need a differential because when they are driven around a tight bend the outside wheel has to travel further, and faster, than the inside wheel. The rear wheels of cars with front-wheel drive are mounted independently, so they can spin freely at their own speed.

I climbed back into the retuned van and set off towards Floating Mountain with the rear wheels spinning and a cloud of salt following. This run was quicker, at 161 mph, but, again, I had my foot hard to the floor and the engine had no more to give. The diff lock hadn't made a lot of difference, and the van was unstable for some of the run. It felt like it was going to break into a big sideways slide. Mike Cook had the best explanation for what was causing the van's back end to feel so squirrelly. He said the back of the van was driving the front, but the front was hitting a wall of air that it didn't have the power to break through, so the back then starts trying to overtake the front. It's to do with wind resistance, and the Transit Custom isn't the most aerodynamic vehicle ever built.

Another thing Mike pointed out was that the Transit would have been helped if it had regular rear-facing exhausts to help break up the vacuum behind it. My Transit has side pipes that exit through the sills in front of the rear wheels, because it wasn't built for running at Bonneville.

The van was nowhere near hitting the speeds it had to if we wanted to break the record. It was actually slower than it had been on the road, which had to be down to the increased drag of the salt on the wide tyres. Most salt racers use narrow wheels and specific Bonneville tyres for the minimal amount of drag. It's not like Formula One, where you need loads of grip for intense acceleration and mental braking; Bonneville racers leave the line gently and steadily build up speed. By now the Transit's V6 had been tuned and given enough to make it the most powerful engine Radical had ever built, with about 800 horsepower. I was all for taking the narrower wheels off the rental van – they'd have fit straight on my Transit – but James wasn't keen. He said he didn't know their history – the tyres might have some damage that we couldn't see. I was willing to take the risk, but no one took the suggestion seriously, so I forgot about it.

The van had the big wing on the back, to keep it planted. Mike noticed a lip on it – he called it a gurney lip – and suggested we take it off to try to gain a bit more speed. It was likely to make the handling even more unstable, and I joked that they should get the helicopter started up just in case.

By now James had increased the boost to 1.45 bar (21 psi), and he didn't really want to go any higher than that. James really knows his stuff, and he's only 25. He knows everything about the Life System engine-management system. He emailed the engine's map – all the different settings for ignition, boost and timing – back to Peterborough from the Salt Flats, and we waited while the Radical factory rewrote it, sent it back and James uploaded it.

James suggested getting the van into top gear, then only giving it half-throttle before flooring it for a blast at the timing line. I was taking the engine to the rev limit in every gear while I was going up through the 'box. It felt like the new map had leaned off the fuel ratio, giving it slightly less fuel, because the engine was misfiring a bit. It was demanding more fuel, but we reckoned the fuel pump couldn't keep up. I soon found out I was right about the lip – removing it made the handling even worse. I had to get off the throttle to settle it down, because it felt like it was aquaplaning.

Even with all that, I only hit 163 mph. And now the charge temperature – the temperature of the air and fuel mix going into the engine – had increased. It was in the 60s, when you want it 30 degrees lower. It was because the turbos were working harder, compressing more air. When air is compressed it makes more heat.

James was worried that if we gave it any more boost we could blow the engine, so we called it a day. I could understand why James and North One believed FT13 AFK could break the van record, but I never shared their confidence. There was even talk that what we'd filmed that morning might not make it into the TV programme, so how much had all that effort cost them? Then Andy the soundman said, 'Well, it's the fastest full-size van,' and a light bulb went on over the producer's head. Supervan 2 was a fibreglass body over a racing-car chassis, so he had a point.

Even though we hadn't beaten 177 mph, it was still a great Wednesday morning, and I wasn't feeling down about it. I was disappointed for Radical and the TV lot, because of the effort and expense they'd gone to, but it's only money. I find it easy saying that when it's not mine.

CHAPTER 20

I know I have a bad earth or two

YOU REMEMBER BRIAN? Looks a bit like Don Logan, Ben Kingsley's character from the film *Sexy Beast*. But in chimp form. Well, he doesn't and he isn't, because he's part of my brain, with an added bit of my imagination. He's my inner chimp.

The idea of the inner chimp was first explained to me by Dr Steve Peters in his popular self-help book *The Chimp Paradox*. The chimp is one of three main parts of the brain; the other two, according to Peters, are the human and computer. The chimp area gets the blood flow first, and that lets it react to situations slightly quicker than the more evolved human part of the brain. That can be a problem because the inner chimp deals with things the way animals do, and in a way most humans have moved beyond – or wish they had. So, Peters explains, the inner chimp is aggressive when it feels threatened, it wants to shag to further the species, it wants to have power over others, be the alpha male or female. To realise how that affects people in normal situations, just think about the bloke who doesn't have their inner chimp under control and gets bumped into in a pub and has their pint spilt. They handle it aggressively, not realising that it was just an accident and 20 pence of Carlsberg is nothing to get wound up about. Every argument has some chimp reaction. The inner chimp is also the part of the brain that has you chucking spanners around the workshop when things aren't going right. So understanding your inner chimp and knowing how to keep it on a lead is important.

Brian was such a big part of my life that he had his own chapter in *When You Dead, You Dead*, but something's changed since finishing that book. I've hardly had a peep out of him in 12 months. I'm not that surprised, because I knew what was setting him off. I could feel him rattling the bars of his cage when I came into contact with the bullshit that has been shovelled on some of the bigger motorbike races. If I couldn't get out of the situation I couldn't do much about it, and soon Brian was screaming. Crowds, however friendly they were, would get him going. Even though the Ulster is one of my favourite meetings, the crowds were just getting a bit much for me there. A crowd creates a crowd creates a crowd.

Keeping Brian quiet was helped by not putting myself in positions that would set him off, and that means not attending any motorbike shows, big races or signings. I nearly raced at a classic motorsport show at the NEC, racing flat track as part of the event. I said to Boastie, my mate from Lincolnshire who had organised the dirt-track racing, that I'd turn up and ride my bike if no one advertised that I'd be there. Then the show's organiser started advertising on the internet that I was going, and encouraging folk to buy tickets because I was going to be there. In the end, I was too flat-out building the wall of death bike to go, so I had to duck out of it, but the whole internet thing made the decision easier. Not going wasn't a problem, from my point of view, because no one was supposed to know I was going anyway, but maybe some people bought tickets thinking they might see me. I don't get why they would go to a show just to see me, but I'm sorry if it buggered up their day.

It felt like a big weight off my shoulders when I knew I wasn't going racing, and I wouldn't be asked the same questions again and again while I had to stand there nodding, smiling, agreeing. This isn't me being ungrateful or rude – it's just the way I'm wired up. I know I have a bad earth or two.

The chimp is still there. He, or she, is in most of us. I've always thought that cycling kept him quiet, and even when I was wasting time getting lost on the Tour Divide he didn't affect my mood or decision-making. But I felt Brian waking up for the first time in ages when I was at Bonneville. He was trying to stick his oar into things that didn't concern him: 'I knew that. Why did they say one thing when I knew the other? Why didn't they just listen to me?'

Compared to past Brian behaviour it was nowt, though. I reckon Brian will always be a part of me, but not racing is the biggest change. It's yet another reason why it feels like the right decision.

CHAPTER 21

I don't want anyone to believe the hype

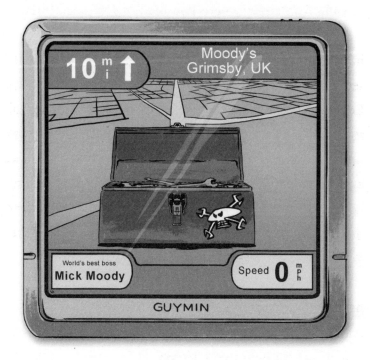

I'D NEVER SAY 2016 was the best year ever, because I don't think of things in that way, and it's only September, so I'm not counting my chickens. But it has been fascinating. I don't plan things too far ahead, and even if I did, if anyone had asked me five years ago about what I'd be doing now, I wouldn't have come up with riding the Tour Divide, trying to break the motorcycle land speed record and racing a V6 Turbo Transit van flat out through Nevada. Who would?

Who else in the world gets the opportunity to do 400 mph on a motorcycle? Very few, and doing that has put me in a circle where I've proved I'm not a messer. Now Matt Markstaller's mate is talking about letting me have a go in a 3,000 horsepower Freightliner truck to see what I think of that. I'm able to talk to people like Ed of Carpenter Racing, who shows me the Triumph streamliner's inlet ports, and it's great because they look nothing like I expected. One thing leads to another, like everything in this book. Who would have thought that talking about tea to some TV bods in 2009 would lead to a programme about the Industrial Revolution to Pikes Peak to Latvia to the wall of death to Bonneville?

So, if I had been asked five years ago about what I'd be doing in the future, I know I would have said, 'Fixing trucks.' And I'm still doing that, thanks to Mick Moody being the best boss in the world.

I thought I'd have a chance to breathe when I stepped out of racing for a while, but I have hardly had time to think. Even though road racing was such a big part of my life for so long, I don't miss it one bit. I look forward to having Sundays to myself now. I take the dog for a walk, spend some time in my shed, sometimes go to the pub for Sunday dinner. There's always been more to me than racing, whether other people believed that or not. For a few years, the Isle of Man TT was the big thing in my life, but I won't go back to racing regular stuff. Right now I'm getting my Martek ready to go race the Burt Munro Classic hill climb in New Zealand, and I'm dead looking forward to it.

I've changed my opinion on the telly stuff too. In the past I thought I wanted to give the TV job a rest, because I felt I was doing too much and getting lost, but I'm not thinking like that so much. A big part of that is because the ideas North One are coming up with are good – they're things I want to do. It's stuff you'd pay to do, but I still want the dog to wag the tail. I'm the dog in this partnership. That's why, when Moody puts his foot down and says I can't go filming, whether it's me that's cocked up the dates or not, I'm not too fussed, even though it does cause grief for Spellman and the TV lot, and I'd prefer not to do that. It does always get sorted, though. This is probably the busiest year I've had with the telly job since the first year, when I took six weeks off work and knocked my teeth out. So I must be doing something right.

I can be awkward sometimes, but it's nothing to do with having been on telly and thinking I can throw my weight around. I'm just a truck mechanic who works for Mick Moody. I don't want people blowing smoke up my arse – I want them telling me to get on with a job, because that's what happens in the real world. I don't want people scared to tell me stuff, because, when it comes down to it, I am only a wanker. When I did that thing in Lincoln, pedalling up and down Brayford Pool in the failed human-powered speed-record boat, hundreds of people lined the waterfront shouting encouragement, and it reminded me that I just do stuff for me, not for pats on the back.

I liked it when I first met Matt Markstaller in Portland. He wasn't talking down to me, but he was telling me how it had to be. He wasn't rude, but he was blunt. He was the same when we met on Bonneville Salt Flats, but a few days later, when I proved I could ride the machine he'd built, he started talking to me differently, and I didn't know why. I have more respect for people when they don't pussyfoot around me. I don't want people to think I'm doing something they can't do, because I don't want anyone to believe the hype.

Sometimes I'm so busy I want it all to stop, but every time I do stop I'm itching to start something else. Like I've explained, even before I finished the Tour Divide I was wondering what was next. I have to find the next thing, but I also like getting back to Moody's.

I was hoping to have had a good go at the land speed record before this book went for printing, but the timings changed because of the condition of the salt, and

I'm finishing this with the dates up in the air. Initially, I thought all I had to do was turn up and open the throttle, but there's a lot more to it than that. I've shown everyone involved that I'm man enough for the job, but everything's got to be right to really go for the record. I like that the limiting factor is now the bike. Up until the end of the first test it had been me, but by the end of that first week I was ready to go faster than it was able to. And I'd gone faster in it than anyone had before.

Wherever I've been and whatever I've been doing, when I get back to the truck yard it's always the same: there will be a note on a toolbox telling me what to do. The first time I speak to Moody, all we'll talk about is what needs doing. He won't ask where I've been or what I've been up to for a couple of days. And I like that. More than that, I need it. Moody doesn't believe the hype, and neither should you.

STOP PRESS

The week before the book went to the printers I was out in Bonneville again with Matt Markstaller and the Triumph streamliner at Mike Cook's Land Speed Shootout. We were hoping to get closer to the record than we had in my first time in it, but the week started off badly with a couple of days of rain. The salt dried out, but it left it very soft and bumpy and not good enough for top-speed record runs. Cars were running and causing big ruts in the track, making the salt look and feel like slushy snow, but I still wanted to get in the thing and build up my experience.

There were a few hold-ups with the streamliner. The FIM tech inspectors picked up on some stuff which held us up. When I asked if my first ride back in the thing could be with the training wheels bolted to the side, Matt told me I didn't need them. I got there on Monday and the first run was Friday afternoon. We set off being towed to the end and in less than two miles I got cross-rutted, couldn't keep it up and the streamliner went down on its side. It only caused cosmetic damage, but we lost a day checking it over. I was out in it the next morning again, but this time it wasn't running right and took another day to sort out.

I'm not patient when I'm waiting for parts at Moody's, but out there you have no choice but to be patient, so I wasn't getting frustrated. You can't make an omelette without breaking eggs, it was just taking a bit longer to clean them up than anyone wanted.

I had one more run before we were set to go home. I accelerated away fine, but got caught in another rut, lost control and barrel rolled the streamliner. I was alright, no bother, but the streamliner had some damage this time, the swingarm got bent, so it was game over.

We learned summat though: if the salt's not perfect, there's not a lot of point in being there, but I want to keep coming back. There is only a certain selection of people who are doing streamliner land speed records: Chris Carr, Rocky Robinson, Valerie Thompson. Who else has the knack? It's a very small bunch of people and I want to be one of them. I want people to think, Get in touch with him, he's not a messer.

Index

GM indicates Guy Martin.
Page references in *italics* indicate illustrations.